Bedtime Stories for Adults:

Soothing Sleep Stories with Guided Meditation. Dive Into Deep Sleep Hypnosis to Prevent Anxiety and Panic Attacks. Let Go of Stress and Relax.

© **Copyright 2019 by Andy Benson - All rights reserved.**

The content contained within this book may not be reproduced, duplicated or transmitted without direct written permission from the author or the publisher.

Under no circumstances will any blame or legal responsibility be held against the publisher, or author, for any damages, reparation, or monetary loss due to the information contained within this book. Either directly or indirectly.

Legal Notice:

This book is copyright protected. This book is only for personal use. You cannot amend, distribute, sell, use, quote or paraphrase any part, or the content within this book, without the consent of the author or publisher.

Disclaimer Notice:

Please note the information contained within this document is for educational and entertainment purposes only. All effort has been executed to present accurate, up to date, and reliable, complete information. No warranties of any kind are declared or implied. Readers acknowledge that the author is not engaging in the rendering of legal, financial, medical or professional advice. The content within this book has been derived from various sources. Please consult a licensed professional before attempting any techniques outlined in this book.

By reading this document, the reader agrees that under no circumstances is the author responsible for any losses, direct or indirect, which are incurred as a result of the use of information contained within this document, including, but not limited to, — errors, omissions, or inaccuracies.

Table of Contents

Table of Contents
Introduction..5
Story 1: Beachside Bonanza...........................10
Story 2: Wedding Bells Ring..........................20
Story 3: How Lucky..35
Story 4: Breaking the Cycle...........................48
Story 5: Road Trip!..61
Story 6: Happy Birthday!...............................74
Story 7: Novel Heights..................................89
Guided Meditation 1: Exploring Time and Space..104
Guided Meditation 2: Peaceful Paradise.......121

Introduction

Stress is something that we all carry within us. We have finances. We have relationships, romantic, personal, and platonic that can weigh on us. We have careers that we have to manage. We have families (possibly). We have responsibilities that force us to act within the world and those can be incredibly exhausting. We can find ourselves barely able to cope with ourselves in these times. In fact, roughly 33% of adults report that they struggle with sleep at any given point in time. They may find that they can't fall asleep. Others find that they can't stay asleep. No matter where you may fall on that spectrum, however, the consequences are real. You can't sleep and you feel *awful*. You feel like you can't successfully get through anything. You find yourself struggling with everything that you do and that is not fair to you. It is incredibly unfair that you find yourself feeling entirely bogged down by your inability to sleep, and all day long, you will struggle to perform up to standard. You won't be able to help yourself or succeed at anything that you need to do.

Sleep is essential to your day. It is imperative to your body and mind. You must be able to sleep at some point, and if you don't get it at night, your body will take it in other ways. Working heavy machinery when tired is dangerous. Driving while having not slept in the last 17 hours creates equivalent impairment to being legally drunk with a blood alcohol level of 0.05% due to the slowing responses that you will have. If you aren't careful, you can find yourself in a serious accident if you are not getting enough sleep to keep yourself well cared for.

Beyond just causing impairment, however, not getting enough sleep is going to make other problems come to light as well. You are going to find that you struggle with being able to function in all aspects of your life. Of course, struggling will only exacerbate those feelings of stress that you have, and that will in turn lead to you getting even less sleep in a constant feedback loop of your own personal struggles. If you want to avoid this problem, you need sleep. Of course, that is easier said than done when you are tired and stressed out! Insomnia tends to repeat itself and make itself worse over time. It can cause you to
seriously struggle by no fault of your own, but you can learn to fix the problem.

This book is here to provide you with a handful of stories that you can enjoy that will help you to gently fall asleep. As you read though this book, you will be treated to two guided meditations and seven different stories that are designed to help you. Those first two meditations are not the traditional bedtime story that you may be accustomed to—these stories are guided meditations. They are meant to help you fall asleep by redirecting your focus. The remaining seven stories are there

If you have read the first book, you know that there were three meditative techniques that were introduced. In this book, you will be introduced to another meditative technique that will be used—this time, we will make use of progressive relaxation to slowly but surely let go of your anxiety and depression or stress that may be holding you back from getting your sleep. You can find that sleep that you are looking for—you just have to learn how to achieve it and this book will help you. You will also be focusing on the mindful concept of acceptance—of being in the moment and not resisting.

Progressive relaxation starts first with a body scan. You will work your way throughout the entire body, bit by bit. You will look at each part of your body to understand what may hurt or where your tension or anxiety is manifesting. Then, with progressive relaxation, you will slowly release it little by little. You will start with your head, feeling your scalp relax first, then your forehead and your other body parts as well. Over time, you will eventually make your way all the way down to your toes to help yourself relax. This involves working over your whole body to leave yourself relaxed and calm so that you can achieve anything that you may want.

Keep in mind that if you currently suffer from anxiety or depression, this book will not magically treat you. It will not make you suddenly un-depressed or un-anxious. This book is not the substitution for a doctor or anything else, either. It is something that you can use to help yourself to alleviate symptoms of anxiety and depression by teaching you how you can relax your body on your own time. You will be empowered to take control of your own body so you can successfully achieve the sleep you have been missing. However, if you find that these techniques do not help you, you may want to consider seeing your doctor for a more thorough checkup to ensure that you are not suffering from something else that is causing the problem.

Relaxation comes from within. If you want to be at peace with yourself, you have to be willing to accept yourself. You have to practice accepting the current moment without resistance. You must help yourself to stop trying to resist what you cannot control. You must sometimes be willing to accept that all there is for you to do is to be at peace. Sometimes, all you can do is remind yourself that you must simply relax and be one with yourself. Sometimes, your anxiety is about things that you cannot fix, and that is what will keep you awake at night. The easiest fix for that is to let go. It is to release that fear and anxiety within yourself so that you can do better. That is what these meditation stories are here to teach you—you will explore worlds and learn that sometimes, you must just focus. Sometimes, you must just go with the flow and see what happens. This is freeing—it will teach you that you don't have to waste your time worrying about things that you have no control over.

Now, if you are ready to get started, a full night's sleep is within your reach—you just have to get started. If you are ready, find your way to your bed, get yourself comfortable, and let's get started. Good night!

Story 1: Beachside Bonanza

Sophie completely forgot that she had agreed to go to the beach with all her friends, and when her good friend Cara shows up, demanding that she goes along with them anyway, even on short notice, Sophie realizes she has no choice! She has to fulfill the beach day promise, and even if she doesn't want to at first, she knows that she'll have a great day doing nothing at all—and it will be worth every moment of it thanks to doing nothing at the beach.

"What do you mean you forgot?!" a young woman, perhaps 25, cried out in disbelief as she stared at Sophie, eyes wide. She had beautiful blue eyes, perfect blonde waves that cascaded down her shoulders, and a perfect fit body. She was the epitome of the beach babe as she sat there, staring at Sophie in shock as she waited for her best friend to explain herself. She was all ready to go already, dressed in a bikini with a thin, lace cover-up and a wrap skirt around her waist. Her sunglasses were perched carefully above her face, and her full lips were in a full pout. "Sophie! If we don't hurry up and leave, we won't get the best spots!"

Sophie grinned sheepishly. "I'm sorry, Cara, I forgot!" she looked around her house. She could probably be ready to go in about fifteen minutes, but she still felt bad. Traffic could get quite bad on those Saturday morning drives out to the beach, especially when the weather was forecasted to be hot. "I can hurry!"

"You better!" Cara frowned playfully at her friend before ushering her away with perfectly manicured hands. Cara was the kind of woman who had to be fashionable in all senses—but fashionably late. She was the kind of person that had to be perfectly punctual everywhere that they went, and if she wasn't 10 minutes early, she was late. Sophie, on the other hand... Now, Sophie was the queen of fashionably late. She was always running behind wherever she went, and whenever she left. She was constantly finding herself battling against the clock, and unfortunately for her, she typically was the loser.

Off Sophie ran, tossing together as many of her beach items as she could into her beach bag, silently thanking the universe that she had felt compelled to shave the night prior. At least that was one thing she didn't have to worry about. Into the bag went her sunscreen, a beach towel, a change in clothes, her favorite book, and a water bottle, and she rushed into her room to change into her swimsuit.

"I'm waiting!!" she could hear Cara cry from downstairs, and she grinned.

"I'm coming!!" she cried back just as loudly. She picked up the bag and barreled back down the stairs as quickly as she could go, but Sophie, ever the ungraceful one, managed to slip near the bottom, crashing down onto her butt and sliding down the final three stairs. "Oof!" she cried out, looking up at Cara. Her cheeks were tinged red with embarrassment and her eyes watered a bit from the pain.

"Shake it off, sweetie, we're going beach bumming!" Cara extended her hand and pulled Sophie up with a smile before she squealed in excitement. "Let's get going! Everyone else will be there soon!"

"I know, I know!" Sophie replied, rubbing her bottom with a sigh. It was just her luck to go to the beach with a bruised tailbone! She rushed out the door and headed toward the car, bag over her shoulder, phone and keys in hand, and ready to go.

An hour later and they were pulling up onto the beautiful white sand of the beach. They were lucky to live in such a diverse area—the mountains were an hour away from one direction, and the beach was the other way, and on that day, she was thrilled to be there. The weather was projected to be 100 degrees all day long, and at the very least, being by the beach would make it bearable if they chose to get into the water. More than anything, however, Sophie was glad to gather up with all of her friends. It had been a while since they had all gotten together, and she was thrilled to have the opportunity to do so for the first time in far too long.

"Oh, great!" Cara called out, raising one hand up as high as she could and waggling her fingers to wave at someone with a grin. "Looks like Lucian, Selah, and Declan are already there. They got a good spot, too! Look—close enough to the snacks, but far enough away that we're not going to be trampled. Good picking, guys!!" The last sentence came out as a squeal of delight as she tried to project her voice toward the other side of the beach. She grinned at everyone. "Aren't we so lucky?"

"Incredibly!" Sophie agreed with a grin. "Let's go!" As soon as their shoes touched the sand, they immediately came off. It was soft and so warm from the sun. Each step caused it to mold around their feet as they sank a little bit, but it was quite pleasant to walk atop. The sun wasn't overwhelmingly hot yet, and the cool ocean breeze brought the temperature just low enough to comfortable. Before long, they were setting up next to their friends, complete with beach umbrellas, plenty of beach towels, a cooler of drinks, and plenty fo excitement for the day.

"Hey, Sophie!" Declan called out with a grin. He was standing there with a grin on his face as he waved at her. He was topless, exposing his impeccably toned and tanned abs, wearing a pair of Hawaiian print swim trunks. Declan's warm, brown eyes met Sophie's gaze and he was genuinely happy to see her as he passed her a cold drink from the cooler. "So, how's the day going?"

"Smashing," Sophie replied with a grin and Cara groaned in mock annoyance at the pun, lightly swatting at Sophie's arm.

"Sophie here just had a bit of an accident this morning. No big deal," Cara chimed in. "Why don't you tell them about it?"

And suddenly, all eyes were on Sophie as she looked at her friends. They were eager to hear what she had to say, and she sighed. "It was no big deal—I slid down the bottom of my stairs, that's all."

Lucian winced in response, flashing a sympathetic smile. "You okay?"

"Yeah, fine!" Sophie replied. "So, what's the plan for the day?"

"Just this," Declan replied, stretching out on his towel. "Lots of R&R out here while we soak up some waves.

"We could go play volleyball!" chimed in Selah.

"Or... *you* could go play volleyball, and we'll cheer you on," Lucian replied, and everyone laughed. It was great to be there, relaxing and no one was quite ready to get out and get sweaty yet. They would much rather spend the time just enjoying the moment of peace.

Selah settled back down onto her towel. "What, Luce, too afraid I'll wipe the floor with you?"

"Something like that," he replied through a sip of his drink. His eyes glowed with laughter as he looked at her. Lucian and Selah had been dating for some time at that point, and they were a great couple together—lots of teasing, but Sophie could tell they genuinely cared for each other.

"Well, I don't know about you guys, but I think I'm interested in some sunbathing, and then maybe burying Lucian in the deepest hole we can manage. Although, it'll be kind of hard to bury that level of ego!"

"Ooh, Sophie, I'm hurt!" he replied with a faux scandalized look on his face.

"Not as much as Sophie's butt!" Declan tossed in, and they all laughed for a moment. It sure was great to be back together, Sophie noted. She was thrilled that they got this opportunity together.

The group fell into a comfortable silence at that point. Sophie was sprawled across her towel, positioning it in the sun at the moment. She was lying, stomach down, simply watching the waves come in and out. Sometimes, it was just fun to people watch while sitting about, and she was thrilled to have that chance.

The ocean itself was shining a beautiful deep blue color, reflecting the sun off of the ripples and waves as it gently lapped up on the shore, rhythmically creating that heartbeat of the song of the beach. The water went on endlessly onto the horizon, meeting the deep blue sky along the way. There was not a cloud in the sky that day—just blue as far as the eye could see up until the sandy beach, covered in rainbow umbrellas, towels, and people wearing every color imaginable. Along with the sounds of waves, Sophie could hear the piercing cries of the seagulls, and the squeals of laughter of both adults and children alike. The sound of music could be heard in the distance and she could tell that the entire day was going to be great. A day at the beach was always a day of leisure, and even if she never moved from that spot, she knew that she would be satisfied with herself and the entire situation. She knew that the day would be a total win if she could sit there just a little bit longer.

As the sun warmed her back, she watched a group of children not too far from where she was sitting. They were happily building a sand castle where they stood, carefully scooping up wet sand into their buckets that they had brought with them. The sand, when wet, was almost the color of brown sugar, she noted, and stuck together about as much as well. She watched them as they worked to pack it in and then carefully place the lump of sand right into place. Their castle was quite intricate—it was clear that they had done this a few times. It had four big pillars, connected with carefully hand-sculpted walls. All around the castle was a great, big moat that they had filled with water, and they had even constructed a carefully built drawbridge with driftwood that they could push over and allow their small collection of action figures to cross at will. The castle was even decorated with all sorts of different items as well—there were seashell windows and a few sand dollars that were being used as decorations at the top as well, and a couple of seagull feathers as flags. All in all, it was quite creative.

Soon, Sophie found her attention drifting to the nearby volleyball game. They were sitting somewhat near a net, likely thanks to Selah's preferences and affinity for the game. She noticed that Selah was over there, too—Selah was petite with deep black hair, great curves, and bronzed skin, and she was fantastic at volleyball. She never ceased to remind everyone about her own experience playing in high school and college, and she continued to play at her local gym as much as she could as well. Sophie watched as Selah got a few great spikes in and wiped the floor with the opposing team, while Lucian was cheering for her from his position as well.

Sophie smiled as she heard him cheering for her—she was so glad to know that he liked her as much as he did. Lucian had always been the bachelor buddy—the one that they all bet would never get married or even settle down into a serious relationship. Seeing him do so was a breath of freshwater.

Her attention drifted again, back to the waves. There was a group of people playing in the waves, and further out at sea, she could see tiny fins, brightly colored. They were sails for boats, all far out at sea, probably fishing for something. There were also people jet skiing, surfing, and floating about. There were children splashing around, squealing happily, in the waves, and people who appeared to be completely uninterested in going in the water at all. It was always interesting to see the different people, Sophie told herself.

"Honey, you have to roll over, or you're going to be well done on your back!" Cara was peering down at her, over her shades. She raised a brow at her friend and used one hand to gesture for Sophie to roll over. "Well? What are you waiting for?" Sophie grinned and groaned and rolled to the front. It was nice to get her back out of the sun, but now, she realized, it was too bright to do anything at all but close her eyes.

So, Sophie shut them, basking in the sun. She allowed the sunlight's warmth to bask over her, covering her in the light that is produced. It was just comfortable, teetering on too hot and it was relaxing. She found herself growing more and more relaxed as she sat there, soaking up the rays, and she didn't really want to get up at all—she just wanted to keep enjoying the moment.

As she sat there, she listened to the sounds of the beach once more, slowly turning her attention to the sound of her breath coming in and out. It was gentle and slow as it came, and she could tell just from the sound of her breath alone that she was feeling highly relaxed. She was ready to enjoy her moment.

Story 2: Wedding Bells Ring

Who doesn't love love? Sophie is thrilled to go to her good friend's wedding, and she is so happy for the lovely couple. She spends her day rushing to get ready, thrilled to enjoy the moment and watch as two more people in the world declare their love for each other and decide that they are going to commit to a lifetime of togetherness. It's so beautiful!

Sophie was up before her alarm for once. She found herself lying in bed, looking out the window. The sun was already up and shining in the sky, and there was not a cloud in sight. It was a perfect day for an outdoor wedding, and that was exactly what they were going to have that day. Sophie was heading out for the day for a local destination wedding—she and a dozen of her friends were all going to be out at an island only accessible by ferry for a beautiful wedding, followed by a day staying in a few of the local bed and breakfasts before everyone made it back to the mainland. They were only maybe an hour from home, but they were so separated by virtue of needing to take the ferry to get there that it felt like a far off destination wedding. It was going to be exciting and beautiful, and a real testament to their love. Sophie was thrilled to see it. She knew that it would be a fantastic wedding, complete with plenty of love and happiness. They didn't need to have some extravagant wedding far from home—just the small, cozy ceremony would be enough for them and it was perfection as far as Sophie was concerned. What was more intimate than enjoying the day with your closest friends and the family that you love?

Sophie was excited to see that testament to love. She was confident that it would be great—it would be just as perfect as she was imagining and she honestly couldn't wait. Though Sophie wasn't married herself and even though she hadn't come even close to finding her own special someone in her life, she knew that she would eventually and she found great joy in watching other people around her get it. She loved to see what people's lives were like after they married and she was confident that she would have a fantastic time listening to everyone else.

She pushed herself out of bed and went straight to the shower. The wedding party would be getting ready to go at the island, but she knew that she should at least be presentable as possible on the ferry. After all, the ferry had a nice café, and she figured that she and her friends would all be stopping to get some coffee while they waited on the thirty minutes that it would take to get there. So, shower, a nice sundress, and makeup it was before she left for the ferry.

It didn't take her long to be ready to go—she just had to wash her hair, throw on a basic amount of makeup, and get dressed to go. She spent maybe thirty minutes in all preparing, putting on a pink dress. It had short sleeves, and the material flowed all around her. There were small red flowers printed across the fabric to accentuate it, and the color went perfectly with her skin and hair. It made her look warmer, more vibrant, and more alive than she had been, and it looked great if she didn't say so herself.

The journey to the ferry terminal took all of thirty minutes, and when she pulled into the line with her car, she was ready to go. She pulled out a book that she had been reading. It was a riveting tale of star-crossed lovers who fought against the odds to be together. Though Sophie wasn't much for romance in her day to day life, she couldn't help it: She was a romantic at heart. She loved being able to see these beautiful proclamations of love, and she loved reading about the romanticized versions of life as well.

Eventually, the ferry was loaded up, and she got the message from her friends—head inside the cabin for a quick drink at the café. So, off Sophie went, leaving her book in place and heading inside. All of her friends were there, huddled around a table near a window that overlooked the beautiful blue water that they were crossing. Sophie took a seat next to Cara and Selah. Around the table, there was also Lindsay, Freya, and Alyssa. They had all been friends since college and stuck to being able to spend time together. Lindsay was a pediatrician in a nearby city. She was married with plans to adopt children in the near future. Freya was happily single as well, with no intention of settling down. She was enjoying the off-beat artist's life, painting and selling her services and pieces of art to local cafes and restaurants. She did quite well, and she figured that children would only slow down her lifestyle. Alyssa was a preschool teacher who loved children. She was the bride to be, and she looked *amazing*.

Alyssa was fair-skinned—she looked as though she might burn if she were out in the sun for longer than twenty minutes. Her features were soft and almost ethereal as she smiled serenely, light shining in from the window nearby. She had soft blue eyes and pale blonde hair, and she was quite dainty in appearance. Her eyes were shining with excitement, and Sophie could tell that she was *thrilled* to be heading to her wedding destination.

"Are you ready?" asked Cara, feigning concern. "After all, as soon as the day is over, you're off the market. *Forever*." She laughed with a smile on her face, and Alyssa returned it. Of their friends, Alyssa was by far the shyest of the group. She was happy to be there with them all, but she was always happiest watching everyone else enjoy themselves without feeling the pressure to really engage with them too much. She was there as added support, but she was definitely one of the best listeners in the group.

She was beloved for this reason—she was like the group mother that always had answers whenever they got stuck doing something that they couldn't get through. She was greatly appreciated for her work because of that, and none of the group could imagine life without her.

"It'll be great!" Alyssa said, smiling shyly. "Thank you for coming. Really. It means a lot that you're all here with me. I couldn't imagine it any different than this."

"Of course, we're here. We love you!" Freya said, patting her on the shoulder. "You're one of our best friends!"

The others echoed the sentiment, nodding their heads emphatically. They were thrilled to see her there, and they were perfectly content being there.

Alyssa blushed and looked down in response. She hadn't really expected that from her friends, and that made her happy to hear. Sophie reached across the table to hold her hands. "We're happy for you."

The girls all chitchatted together as the ferry made its way across the water, and before they knew it, they were pulling into the dock and being instructed to get into their cars and drive off. They were planning on meeting at the local country club, one of the few places on the island that had something other than trails. The island itself was quite small, and there were only a few buildings there. There were only about 600 houses across the entire island, a single small one-stop-shop with one little gas pump, the restaurant, and the one country club for the island members that people are visiting could also rent.

It was a beautiful island, Sophie discovered as they drove off. The whole island was plush with growth, and it hardly felt like they were in a town at all. All of the island was said to be one small town, but to Sophie, it felt more like a forest paradise, separated from the hustle and bustle of the mainland while still be close and accessible if they needed to go to it. It was almost picturesque, feeling like it was more of a movie scene than anything else, and yet they were there.

The club was on the opposite end of the island—they drove across the whole thing, a whole six miles and without a single stop light, all the way to the club. There was a large marina that spanned across the entirety of the shore there, overlooking a beautiful scene of nothing but blue ocean. Puget Sound was technically part of the sea and connected all the way out to the ocean. Whales were known to go through the area that they were overlooking. While it didn't look like there were any whales at that moment in time, they also knew that there was a chance that there could be.

Inside the club was a big community room. It wasn't anything fancy, but it had plenty of space for a meal for all of them to enjoy, and it looked great. Inside the room, there were two long banquet tables, topped with white tablecloths and small bouquets of baby's breath and pale pink roses placed every few place settings. There were maybe 20 in all setup— enough for the guests and the bride and groom. It was definitely a small setup, but each white plate was beautiful ceramic, carefully etched, and molded to create a beautiful design of delicate flowers all along the rims. Each chair was carefully pushed in, with white tulle bows tied at the back. There were strings of lights in a soft white hanging above them, sparkling in the sunlight. Sophie was certain that when they were turned on later, they'd look fantastic, glimmering, and providing a gentle glow to the evening.

They were ushered around, with people who were planning and organizing getting everything going. Sophie found herself very quickly in a room in the back of the club that she was being done up in. Each of the women who were attending the wedding was in there, getting their hair done and their makeup put on. Sophie changed into her dress, a beautiful champagne colored mermaid style dress, hugging her waist and flaring out at the end. The top was lace and the fabric itself was a soft, silky material. It was comfortable, breathed well even in the summer heat, and she thought she looked great.

Sophie looked at herself in the mirror and smiled as she tied her hair up into a loose bun, and she perfected her makeup on her face as well. She was satisfied with how she looked and turned to see how everyone else was doing. Everyone looked great and so far, there was no drama at all. Everything was going perfectly so far and she was thrilled.

Before long, they were all gathering up and congregating at the location for the wedding ceremony. They were going to a point in the island that overlooked the water. They were surrounded by trees, beautifully verdant all around them. There was a wedding arch painted white, covered in flowers all around it. It was gorgeous and underneath it was space for the bride and groom. There were a handful of chairs all positioned in front of it, and quickly, they were all filled up. It didn't take long for everyone to get settled, and then the music started.

As soon as the wedding music began, heads turned. The groom, a man named Alex, walked down the aisle in his suit. He wore a fitted black jacket over his vest and white shirt. His slacks matched perfectly, and his tie was a beautiful maroon color. He had a white rose pinned to his lapel as well as he settled down on one end of the wedding arch. There was an officiant standing there in the center of the arch, waiting for them. Then, Alyssa came down the aisle. She stepped out, looking absolutely stunning. Her hair was allowed to cascade behind her, lightly waved, but free to flow. Her makeup was impeccable—she looked almost unworldly with how beautiful she looked. Her dress had a nice deep v neck plunge, curving to wrap around her breasts, and lace sleeves. The waist was tucked in, and the tulle and chiffon body of the dress shimmered in the sunlight as it wrapped around her, flowing in the gentle breeze. Her shoes were a light silver strapped sandal with small heels. In her hands was a beautiful bouquet, with white calla lilies and deep red roses, along with a few clusters of baby's breath. She held the bouquet up to her chest as she walked down the aisle shyly, the faintest hints of a blush staining her pale cheeks as she did. Her lips were parted ever so slightly as she gazed at her groom, smiling as they locked eyes.

Alex was almost dumbfounded as he saw his bride. His eyes widened, and his smile grew across his face. He couldn't take his eyes off of her as she approached him. Sophie could have sworn she saw tears spring to his eyes as he was finally able to see her for the first time. Sophie always loved watching the groom's reactions to seeing their soon-to-be wives—it was always so pure seeing the sudden rush of emotion in their faces, and she was always so excited to watch on.

As Alyssa made her way to her groom, everyone stared with wide smiles. They joined hands together, and Sophie could see Alex whisper something to Alyssa that she couldn't quite make out, but judging by her teary-eyed smile, she was happy to hear it.

The officiant smiled at the couple. He had a book in his hand, glanced at the paper, then back up at the crowd before he began to speak. "We are gathered here today to witness the union of Alex and Alyssa. Welcome, all! Today is the beginning of a lifelong journey for this couple, and you are here to witness it. Through their mutual love, trust, and respect, they have chosen to live their lives together, embarking on the next major chapter. We are here to celebrate the love and light that we can all see in their relationship, sending them off and wishing them well on such a joyous occasion."

The officiant looked back and forth once more. "So, if anyone would like to object to the forming of their new union, speak now, and forever hold your peace." He looked around the crowd expectantly as Alex and Alyssa tore their eyes away from each other to glance at their audience. The wedding attendants chuckled but remained silent, and both the bride and groom smiled. Sophie wasn't surprised at the lack of objections—they were like the perfect couple for each other, and she was so happy they were finally making it official.

The officiant nodded his head sagely in acceptance. "Perfect, then let's get started!" He looked to the couple once more. "Marriage is one of the most integral parts of our lives as people. As we stand here, we acknowledge that the vows that you are about to take are amongst the most important of your life. They are vows that we have honored throughout the generations, recognizing the real commitment that comes with the declaration of husband and wife. And today, we are here to witness this for Alex and Alyssa. We are here to recognize the choices that they have made to bind together, to enter this union of marriage, to share all aspects of themselves with each other. Today, we witness two individuals becoming one to each other. Now, let's hear from the couple as they recite their vows for each other." The officiant fell silent and nodded to Alex.

Alex looked nervous at first, but he turned his attention to Alyssa, and all of his fear melted away. "Alyssa, I love you with all my heart. You are a beautiful person, inside and out, and I love how you can bring out the best in me, even when I'm at my worst. I love just how loving you are, and how you're the kind of person to stop and help anyone that you see in need. You're that beacon of light that guides me home when I'm lost, and that soft space for me to land. You're everything I've ever dreamed of and more. I promise to you that I will love you, protect you, and cherish you to the best of my ability. You make me a better man, Alyssa, and I vow to help you become the best version of yourself that you can be as well." He smiled at her, and Sophie could see him squeeze her hands.

Alyssa was watching him with teary eyes, smiling. At the moment, all she was focused on was her partner, and the entire crowd was silent as they watched the tender moment. The officiant nodded to Alyssa to get her to start her own vows.

"Alex, I promise to love you and honor you every day of my life. I promise to be your biggest cheerleader as you make your way through the world, and the one to help you when you're at your lowest. I promise to help you as much as I can and to raise you up. I will always do my best to help you and to cherish you. I promise to support you in any way I can." She blushed as she spoke, and Sophie could see the tears springing to both Alex and Alyssa's eyes as she did.

They fell silent and gazed into each other's eyes for a moment, smiling tearfully at each other.

The officiant smiled at them both. "Now, Alex, Alyssa. It's time to join hands." He waited for them to intertwine their fingers with each other. "Alex, in front of friends and family that

31

have gathered here today, you are preparing to take Alyssa as your lawfully wedded wife. Are you ready?

"Yes."

"Alyssa, are you ready to accept Alex as your husband?" The Officiant turned to look at her.

"Yes," she replied quietly.

"Alex, do you take Alyssa as your lawfully wedded wife, to love and cherish from this day forward, to have and to hold in sickness and in health, for better or for worse, for richer or for poorer, until death do you part?"

"I do," Alex said, his voice barely above a whisper.

"And Alyssa, do you take Alex as your lawfully wedded husband, to love and cherish from this day forward, to have and to hold in sickness and in health, for better or for worse, for richer or for poorer, until death do you part?"

"I do," she replied softly.

The officiant nodded with a soft smile. "Wedding rings are a traditional symbol of the bond, the never-ending commitment, and the strength of the relationship of two soulmates. The bond is unbroken, continuous, and endless in a perpetual circle. By wearing these rings that represent your perfect union, you will always be reminded of the connection that you share, as well as the vows made out of love today." He passed one ring to Alex and one to Alyssa. He dropped his voice down lower and began to recite something that Alex began to copy.

"I, Alex, present to you, Alyssa, this ring as a symbol of our everlasting love and of the vows I have made to you. Let it never lose its luster, just as my love for you will never fade." He gently slid it onto Alyssa's finger with a smile on his face.

Alyssa then began to speak as well: "I, Alyssa, preset to you, Alex, this ring as a symbol of our everlasting love and of the vows that I have made to you. Let it never lose luster, just as my love for you will never fade." And with that said, she slid a ring onto Alex's finger as well.

The officiant smiled at the couple. "And with that, by the powers vested in me by the state, I now pronounce you husband and wife! You may now kiss the bride!"

Alex reached forward and pulled his new wife close, kissing her gently on the lips as her hands snaked behind his neck to embrace him. They lingered a moment as the audience cheered. Sophie clapped and cheered for the new happy couple as she watched them.

As they separated, smiling at each other happily, with Alyssa's cheeks blushing, the officiant said, "Ladies and gentlemen, I now present to you, Mr. and Mrs. Johnson!"

Story 3: How Lucky

Sophie meets someone new! Sparks are flying after Sophie runs into someone new while taking a walk with Bella through the park one fine autumn afternoon. She wasn't expecting it, but she couldn't deny the chemistry between them. She's happy to spend her day with him, though!

An autumn chill clung to the breeze that flew by. It smelled of that musky, earthy, sweet scent of leaves as they started to fall, and the leaves all around in all of the trees were a warm yellow. The trees were lit up with color, glowing with red and orange hues that spread across the entire area. It was a beautiful sight to behold as Sophie walked down the park trail with Bella at her side. Sophie wore a beige jacket that fell down to her mid-thighs with black buttons along with it. She wore a loose white shirt, covered up with an oversized orange scarf. Her pants were so dark blue that they were practically black, and she wore a pair of grey tie-up boots as well.

Next to her, Bella was perfectly content to walk along. She was well behaved, walking right next to Sophie. She was happy to follow along without a problem—she wanted to enjoy her walk through the park. She just wanted to go about her day. The dog was really quite well trained, all things considered, and she loved to follow along obediently. She was content the most when she was able to enjoy a nice leisurely walk. She didn't even really enjoy being forced to run around.

At the very least, Sophie told herself, walking around in the autumn air meant that between warming herself up moving around and the air chilling her off, she was very comfortable as they wandered through the trails. They were walking along a nice urban park, filled up with plenty of greens, grass, trees, and sidewalks with the occasional bench that could be sat on. It was a beautiful park that was clean, safe, and enjoyable, and because it was the middle of a school day, it was quiet enough without children playing around. She loved that she was free to go about her day as if nothing was going on. The sheer pleasantries were enough for her to feel perfectly content.

Sophie wasn't expecting anything but an ordinary day. She certainly didn't know what was in store for her, and she certainly wasn't expecting what happened next.

Out of nowhere, Bella stopped, perked her head up, sniffed at the air, and bolted away, tearing the leash out of Sophie's gentle grasp. Bella *never* ran off like that—she never bothered to hold onto the leash very tightly because she had never felt the need to do so. She took off running as far away as she could with no indication of stopping. Sophie was shocked, to say the least. She was definitely not dressed for a jog through the park—she wasn't even sure that her boots would allow her to run! But, the desire to not lose her dog outweighed the discomfort of trying to run in such un-athletic clothing, and off she went as quickly as possible. She ran ad ran as fast as her legs would allow in such unsuitable clothing. However, Bella could not be deterred. She seemed determined to find something as she ran, and the faster that she went, the harder that Sophie felt she needed to run.

Sophie was panting and sweaty by the time that Bella finally stopped. She was sitting under a beautiful tree that was alight with color. The beautiful oranges and yellows across the branches were gorgeous. The pup was sitting there perfectly—she was looking up at Sophie as if she had done exactly what she had been commanded to do. She sat there with a doggy grin on her face, tail curled perfectly along her haunches as she waited for Sophie to catch up.

"Bella!!" Sophie gasped out as she stopped, resting her hands onto her legs. "What has gotten into you?" She looked down at the dog with an almost exasperated expression as she ran her hand through her hair. "You usually never run away, girl. Why this time," Of course, she wasn't expecting an answer in return as Bella stared up at her with that self-satisfied, wolfish grin. Her tongue was lolling out to the side of her mouth, and she twitched an ear in response as if she knew exactly what she was doing. "At least I got my workout in for the day..." she murmured to herself as she picked up the leash from the ground. It was dirty and covered in little bits of leaf litter that stuck to the nylon length while Bella dragged it through the soil. At least it wasn't wet; she told herself as she picked it up delicately, wrinkling her brows at it as she did.

As Sophie stood up, she saw someone staring at her, and she froze. He was looking at her quizzically, one perfect eyebrow arched right over his warm, brown eyes. He was confused at her outburst, perhaps, or he simply found it fun to start at or accost women that were having a hard time. Sophie opened her mouth to speak up but found herself staring at the man instead. He really wasn't bad looking, and as soon as their gazes met, she felt her pulse quicken. She found herself wondering who this person was—she wanted to know everything.

And in that moment, Sophie had to wonder if there was such a thing as fate after all.

She could feel her heart thudding against her ribs so hard that she had to wonder if they were going to break. What should she do? What should she say? Would she need to change what she was doing? Should she say something at all, or would it be better if she waited for him to speak to her? It was hard to know what was right and what she should do when her mind felt so foggy she couldn't think.

Sophie wasn't usually like this—she was not one to be swayed by this idea of love, nor was she the kind of person who believed in love at first sight—but she was definitely feeling *something* in the moment. She opened her mouth to speak, breaking their eye contact as she glanced at the ground, but before she could say a word, she heard him speaking instead.

"Are you okay?"

She looked back up at him in surprise. Okay? She was fine! Yeah, she was a bit sweaty and disheveled from chasing after her partner in crime, but she was doing a lot better than she could have been. After all, she could have been hurt, or Bella could have been lost. "Do I look like I'm not okay?" she blurted out, immediately kicking herself for what she had to say in response as soon as the words left her mouth. *How embarrassing.*

She heard him chuckle in response. "No, no, it's not that. Just... You're looking a little tense is all." He smiled kindly at her. "I just figured I'd ask. You know, it's not every day you see people running down the park in that. You don't exactly look like you're dressed to jog."

He had a point there, and she nodded, running a hand through her hair in an attempt to tame it and smiling sheepishly. "Yeah... *Someone* decided it would be a good idea to take off on a marathon around the park."

Then, Sophie realized that he was standing there with his own dog. She had been so caught up in looking at his eyes and face that she hadn't even thought to look anywhere else yet. She looked down and saw a grey husky with the most vivid blue eyes that she had ever seen sitting next to him patiently. He was exceptionally well behaved for a husky, just sitting there without so much as moving, though he couldn't keep his eyes off of Bella. "Looks like you might understand my predicament a bit more than I thought, huh?" Sophie asked, laughing. "And what's this big fella's name?"

"This big man here is Koda," he said, patting the husky on the head. "He's surprisingly agreeable today, it looks like." The man smiled affectionately at the dog, and Sophie felt her heart swell as she saw him. She felt her cheeks tinge pinkish as she looked at him, and she looked back down at the dog to look away from the handsome man in front of her. "And my name is Felix."

The man, apparently named Felix, looked at Sophie expectantly, and it took her a moment of looking back at him to figure out what he wanted. Her name! Of course, he was waiting for her to tell him her name as well. Right—that's what she was supposed to do when someone introduces themselves to you. *Get it together, Sophie,* she told herself.

"I'm Sophie, and this is Bella. It's really nice to meet you, Felix," She patted Bella's head in a very similar way. This was nice—she wasn't just saying it. Sophie was happy to have that interaction, but she still wasn't sure what she was supposed to do about the situation that she was in. It was weird to suddenly be in this position in which she had no idea what she was doing, or whether she needed to be able to run away, engage in a longer conversation, or anything else. She didn't know how to feel about this tall, dark, and handsome stranger in front of her.

Felix nodded his head thoughtfully, his gaze softening as he looked at Sophie for a moment. Sophie could have sworn she saw a hint of laughter hidden beneath their warm depths, but it was quickly forgotten when Bella licked her hand, shocking her back to the present.

"Do you normally walk around here?" he asked her, letting his hands slide into his pockets naturally as a cool breeze flew by. It was chilly outside, and she couldn't blame him for this. Though usually, hands in the pockets were a bad sign, she had to admit that she wanted to do the same thing. It was cold!

"Not really. I was just a bit bored and needed a change in scenery. It's quite pretty here. Much better than just staring at my home garden all day long. It's nice to get out and about sometimes. I work at home, and that gets really boring really quickly when I'm on my own at home without anyone around." She stopped speaking when she realized that she had opened up the floodgates, and the words were flying out. With her eyes widening, she glanced up at Felix shyly. "Sorry," she murmured, looking down. "Sometimes, I just start talking, and I can't get myself to shut up. It's so embarrassing—and I'm doing it again!!" She sighed. "I'm sorry!"

Felix shook his head, eyes shining with amusement. "No, it's fine. I asked, and you answered!" He seemed so incredibly patient as he looked at her, and Sophie felt her heart-melting. She didn't normally feel so attached to men—but she couldn't help it. She just wanted to get to know this guy in front of her. She wanted to know more.

Sophie looked down at the ground, steeling up her resolve. She was going to do it! She was going to ask him for his phone number so they could meet up again! She just had to build up the courage somehow. Her thoughts were racing a mile a minute as she sat there, looking at him.

"Hey, Sophie?" he asked with a kind look on his face.

"Hmm?" She looked up at him, her train of thought immediately cut off.

"I apologize that this is somewhat forward... But could I have your phone number, please?" She was *shocked*. She didn't think that he'd want it—but he did! She nodded her head almost numbly before she could say a word in return.

They exchanged phone numbers and spent some time together, chatting about anything and everything that came to mind. She was perfectly content, getting to know him, and working to understand who he was better. She loved hearing what he had to say and how he said it. His voice alone was like music to her ears, and the longer they chatted, the more she wanted to linger.

Even Bella and Koda got along well. They happily walked next to each other, tongues lolling out. Though both breeds were commonly considered aggressive, there was no way that such goofy faces could be seen as problems as they strolled through the park together. They talked about their jobs and about their goals. They spent time discussing where they grew up and what they did in college. Overall, it was incredibly pleasant, and Sophie was thrilled to finally have a deeper connection with someone. She hadn't planned for it, but the effect was undeniable. She liked him. She wasn't sure if she liked him as more than a friend, but she definitely felt that magnetic pull toward him that she couldn't ignore. She wanted to be around him.

Eventually, the sun was starting to set, and they realized that they had spent the entire day just walking through the park, chatting about life and everything that it has done for both of them. They spent time discussing all sorts of topics that she had never imagined that she would discuss with others, but she wasn't embarrassed. No, she was thrilled to have that closer connection to someone else, and she didn't want to lose it. When it became clear that they had to part ways, they still dragged their feet, but eventually, Sophie found herself walking home on her own.

As she walked home, she couldn't help but feel her mind focused on him. She couldn't help but feel like she was on cloud nine the whole time she went along her way. All she thought of was Felix. His warm, brown eyes were almost the color of honey. The look of joy he had when he went about everything he did. The kind smile... He was such a genuinely good guy, and Sophie wanted to get to know him sooner rather than later. She wanted to know that she could trust him, and she was pretty sure that she could.

The entire time she made her way home, she was desperate to hear her phone go off. She was hoping that it would ring in her pocket, that he would text her. She could imagine the whole conversation in her head.

"How are you doing?" he would ask her over the phone. His voice would be gentle, curious, but that small note of longing was unmistakable. She knew that he was just as interested in her as she was of him, and she couldn't erase the feeling.

"I'm good, thanks. How are you doing?" she would ask him back, nervously twirling her hair. Was he thinking about how nervous she was? Was he nervous himself? Her own voice held that slight air of timidity, that fear of being rejected.

"I'm glad I got to hear your voice again," he'd practically purr into the phone line. "You're such a sweet person; you know that, Sophie? I couldn't wait until tomorrow to reach out... I just had to hear from you again." His voice was soft, almost urgent. She could almost feel his fervor in his voice, and she would find herself wishing that she was there...

But, then, something shocked her out of her daydream—her phone was ringing.
She blinked in surprise as if she were just waking up, and she pulled her phone out of her pocket. She was hoping that she would hear him on the other line, but a glance at the name deflated the excitement that she felt within

herself. It was just Cara, ready to hear about her day.

She told Cara all about the day. She told her about Felix, about how sweet he was, and about how much she couldn't wait to hear back from him. She was smitten before she even realized it. Cara laughed at her, telling her that it was definitely a crus and that she had to act upon it sooner rather than later. "He sounds like a good guy," Cara purred into the phone. "You should take him off the market before someone else does. He won't be single forever, it sounds like. You only live once! What are you waiting for, hon?"

When Sophie and Cara got off the phone, Sophie was shocked. Did she like him romantically? Her phone buzzed with a text message, and when she looked down at it, she saw:

Hey, it's Felix, from the park earlier today.

She felt her stomach fluttering in those butterflies that she had not felt since high school, and she realized it. She was totally smitten with him. But did he like her? She wasn't so sure, but she knew one thing: She would be genuinely upset if she couldn't get to speak to him again.

All night long, Sophie and Felix texted. She eventually fell asleep with her phone in her hand, a half-written message there for her to see in the morning, a testament to just how interested in him she was. They had a great conversation, and Sophie felt like they really hit it off. She just had to convince him that they could be wonderful together and give them a shot. The more that they spent time together, the more confident she was that they would enjoy their time together.

Story 4: Breaking the Cycle

Sophie is bored with her routine. Day in and day out, she does the same thing. She gets up, checks her email, does some work, heads out for lunch, comes home, works some more, then gets ready for her peaceful evening at home. It's easy and predictable... But also so drab. She's sick of it. She's ready to do anything that she can to break the cycle and do something new. Something exciting! Variety is the spice of life, and she's ready to find something to spice up her cycle. Join Sophie as she spends a day directly breaking her usual routine to find some excitement and pizzazz to bring back to her life.

Sophie yawned as she poured her coffee. It went right into her usual cup, filled to the brim and steaming. The cup was her typical light, a baby blue mug with the quirky quote engraved on the side: It had a picture of a fox on it and said *'Zero foxes given'* and Sophie loved it. It usually made her smile as she pulled out her coffee mug, but that day, she just sighed. She looked down at the mug with a frown. Something *had* to give. She couldn't take it any longer! Something needed to be different before she lost her mind.

She slammed her coffee mug onto the counter with a clatter and dropped her hands into her face, feeling the frustration and fatigue of the same thing day in and day out wearing at her. She needed something to change, or she would have to *scream!* Something needed to be different! She couldn't take it any longer! She had to change it up before she blew up. "That's it!" she mumbled to herself, looking around her home. Of course, nothing was out of place, other than the tennis ball that Bella had left there for her. Something had to be different. Something needed to change!

She looked down at the counter and realized that some of the brown liquid had splashed out, pooling on the surface, and she sighed, pulling over a paper towel and wiping it up. There had to be something she could do for the day... Anything at all... Into the trash went the paper towel and Sophie pulled out her phone, glancing over her calendar for the day. It was the same as it always was. Work until lunch, then spend some time working on another project after. It was exactly the same as it always was, and she was *sick of it*. With a frustrated eye roll and a sigh, she looked down at the ground. Maybe it was a day of spontaneity. She normally had to work, but she could take care of that the next day instead... she felt like what she needed the most was to go do something exciting and different!

Sophie ran upstairs to get dressed without so much as a plan in mind. She'd figure it out one way or another—she just had to do something. Anything would work that day. Her outfit for the day was simple but practical: She picked out a pair of nice, dark blue jeans that hugged her hips nicely and accentuated her legs. For a top, she pulled out a nice floral blouse that hung loosely around her, flowing as she moved. It was black with soft, pink designs as it hung off of her, and she finished the look with long, knee-height grey leather boots.

Off she went down the stairs after tossing her hair into a loose bun to keep it out of her face. She wasn't quite sure what to do during the day. She wasn't sure if she was going to go shopping, or if she was going to spend her day wandering, or if she would pick up some new books. Whatever she chose to do, however, she knew that it needed to be different. She picked up her purse, walked out the door, and hopped into her car. She sat there and sighed. "I don't know what to do..." she groaned to herself as she started the ignition.

As she drove off, she looked around the neighborhood. She saw a woman pushing a stroller with a dog trotting next to her. They were enjoying the afternoon sun as they walked down the road, and it brought a smile to Sophie's face. She loved being able to watch people happily going about their days. It was fun being able to see other people and imagine what is going on in their minds. She liked seeing what people did in their lives to see what they liked. She loved seeing it all.

The houses were all neatly cared for and the yards were immaculately groomed to be perfect as she drove by them all. The houses all looked quite similar as she went down—they were nice, two-story houses, lined up with big, white, two-car garages in the front and great big bay windows. Each house had a small tree in front of them—they were maple trees that, when fully grown and matured, would shade the sidewalks as people chose to walk through it. The houses were all in nice, warm colors, in tans and browns. They looked great with their perfect, white garages and white front doors, almost as if there was something requiring every house to be made up the same way. As Sophie went through them all, she found herself staring in awe. They were beautiful and the front lawns were immaculate. Each lawn was carefully cultivated, and there were small gardens underneath the front windows. The flowers were beautiful, in bushes with little white ones growing in small clusters. Some of them had great, big hydrangea plants growing, in all sorts of different colors as well. Some were more blue while others erred toward redder shades.

Though the houses all looked quite similar, they had marked differences as well. She could see some that had bigger windows than others. Some had big window walls, and others had rooms over garages. They had different kinds of porches and different kinds of paths leading to their doors. Seeing the cohesion between the houses made her happy as she went by them all. It was refreshing to see the different ways that the houses come together. It was great to see, especially when the families were outside the house and doing what they do.

Soon, she turned off the road she was on and made her way toward a park down the road. It was a great, big park with trees bigger than any others in the area. The trees had massive canopies, branching out for feet and feet as they shaded the grass underneath them. Sophie loved that park—there was a big playground for kids, but there were also plenty of paths for walking, and lots of grass for sprawling out, for running in, and for having picnics. It was one of the parks that Sophie used to go to with Bella when she was younger—but lately, they had chosen out a different park a bit closer to home.

Briefly, Sophie debated stopping in there to see what it would be like. She looked over everything, only to shake her head. No—she wasn't going to stop in at the park. Today was a day for doing something new. A day for discovering a new sense of self. It was a day for figuring out what she wanted to do at the moment—for spontaneous decisions, and that was what she would do, and she would start it all off by trying out that new sushi restaurant at the mall that she had meant to go to.

The sushi restaurant wasn't too far away, and she knew that she could get there quickly—she just had to drive down a couple of miles, and she'd get there. She turned up the music, bopping her head along to the beat as she drove, a big grin on her face. She looked forward to that new sushi restaurant—all she had to do was drive a little bit further, and she'd get there. She had heard it was one of those fancy conveyer belt sushi places where you took half a roll at a time and got to mix and match your plate into exactly what you wanted. She always really liked those ones—you could try something and get only a couple of bites without having to worry about the cost when you tried something new. She loved picking out a new dish or a new type of fish every single time. The last time she had gone to a sushi restaurant, she tried the eel, and it had been surprisingly delicious. It had been a bit intimidating to go out of her way to try it, but she was certainly willing to give it a shot just to say she had. After all, trying something new every day was a great thing-- everyone always recommended it, after all.

Within a few minutes, she found herself pulling into the parking lot, and she grinned. She was *starving*. She stared at the sushi restaurant, aptly named "Sushi Belt" and on the sign, she could see a cute, cartoonized roll of sushi wearing a big belt across its waist, sitting on a plate on another belt. It was something adorably delicious to look at and just made her even hungrier as she walked off on her way.

The parking lot was surprisingly empty, but that wasn't too surprising. It was still early for lunch, and the restaurant was only just then opening. She went into the restaurant and took a seat at a single bar, plopping her purse next to her. A waitress quickly brought her a menu and handed her a glass of water before stepping away. She looked at everything in front of her, watching the little plates go by. Each plate had a different color around the rim, marking it as worth a different amount from the others. There were five colors in all, and each had different foods. The cheapest ones were covered in edamame, sautéed green beans, and egg rice balls. The most expensive ones touted shrimp, crab, and salmon. There were pieces that were simply raw fish on plates. There were other pieces that were rolled into nice pieces and cut carefully. Others still were lumped onto balls of sushi rice. The different options went by at a gentle pace, with the occasional plate of fresh fruit, seaweed salad, and miso soup passing by as well.

The restaurant smelled great, and Sophie looked over the menu. There was bound to be something interesting to try new that day—she just had to choose something out. As the food went by, she picked up a few of her favorites— she grabbed a seaweed salad with little sprigs of green onion and sesame seed sprinkled atop it, and a bowl of miso soup. She picked out a few regular plates of sushi as well—grabbing a

California roll, a spider roll, and a plate of seared tuna.

The meal looked great, and as she broke her chopsticks, she considered what she would be doing next. She could go see a movie... or she could head over to the mall for some shopping. But, neither of those seemed all that exciting to her when she had so many other things to do as well. Well, she told herself as she picked up a piece of California roll and popped it into her mouth, enjoying the savory crab salad within it as she watched the lazily revolving sushi bar spin around and around in front of her, she could do just about anything that day. It didn't matter—she just needed to choose something.

Before long as she went along, she realized something: their octopus on the menu. She had never tried it before—the strange tentacle shape always put her off from the idea of even trying it, and she cringed to think of the suckers on them clinging to her lips as she tried to chew it up. She frowned as she debated it for a moment, but then something overcame her— she was going to do it. She *had* to do it. She wanted to reclaim her independence and reclaim her ability to do new things. It wouldn't be the worst thing she had ever done, after all— and she had to try something new.

When the waitress came by again, she strengthened her resolve. When she was asked if she wanted anything else, she nodded her head. "Yeah, actually... Could I try the octopus?" She smiled at the waitress, but she was certain her apprehension was received loud and clear from the woman, who smiled politely and nodded her head.

"Sure thing, hon." She walked off after filling up Sophie's water again and left Sophie to her meal.

The seaweed salad tasted great as she turned to that, enjoying each and every piece in front of her. She loved it: It tasted better here than at the other restaurants she had gone to as well. It was perfectly salty, delicate, and delicious. As she thoughtfully chewed it through, she wondered what the octopus would be like, hoping that it wouldn't be tough or anything. She didn't want to feel like she was chewing on a rubber or something. Next came a sip of her miso soup, which was warm and made perfectly.

As Sophie slowly and thoughtfully ate at her food, the waitress returned, placing it right next to her and leaving her to it. She looked at the octopus as it sat on the plate, apprehensive about what to do next. Obviously, she had to take a bite of it—but she was hesitant. She wasn't sure she really was ready for it. She wasn't sure that it would be worth it. The tentacles were curled slightly on their plate, and she could see the suckers. She was thankful the tentacles had been removed prior to the food being cooked. That was perfect for her—she wasn't sure she would have been able to stomach it if the octopus had been entirely whole when it was presented for her. She looked at it closely and studied the color. It was orange-ish with tiny white suckers alongside it. There were three tentacles left onto the plate for her, and she wasn't quite sure where to begin. Before she thought much more about it, however, she simply grabbed one tentacle with her chopsticks and popped it into her mouth. It was surprisingly tender as she chewed it up, and the taste wasn't too much, unlike lobster, she decided as she carefully chewed it up. It was surprisingly decent as she ate it. In fact, it was so decent that she decided to have a second bite as well. She even ate the third bite, too, finishing the plate. She was glad she had taken the chance and tried it—it was delicious.

As she finished eating her meal, someone popped into the chair next to her. She was another woman, all on her own, simply enjoying the moment, from what Sophie could tell. She smiled and waved at Sophie as she sat down. She was an older woman with salt-and-pepper hair and with a kind look to her face. There were wrinkles from smiling and laughing around her mouth, but it really just added to her kind look of authenticity, Sophie decided as she popped another piece of sushi into her mouth.

Just then, the waitress came by. "So, you liked the octopus, eh?" she asked as she peeked in to see if Sophie was done eating.

"Yeah, actually. It was surprisingly good!" she replied to the waitress with a smile. "I didn't expect to enjoy it so much, but it was great!" She was genuinely shocked that she liked it that much, but stranger things have happened, after all. As the waitress left, the woman sitting next to her looked at her.

"You tried the octopus?" she asked, sounding impressed.

Sophie nodded, feeling her cheeks flush a bit in embarrassment. "It was surprisingly good," she replied with a grin. She watched the woman see what her reaction was. "It tasted kinda like lobster," she told her. "I really enjoyed it. It could have been a lot worse than it was, that's for sure."

"What made you try it?"

"I figured I'd try something new. You know, do something new, or frightening once per day and all." She shrugged her shoulders. "I wasn't sure how I'd feel, but you'll never know how you feel about something until you try it, and that's what I did. It could have been much, much worse, that's for sure. But, you know what? Now I know I actually do like an octopus. I'm not sure I'd go out of my way to order it form a restaurant again in the future, but I know I wouldn't turn it down if I were offered it." Sophie felt a bit braver already just discussing it. She was proud of herself. That was definitely unexpected.

"Well, good for you! I'm glad you did it. Maybe I'll give it a shot, too," replied the old woman as she glanced through the menu. "I'm sure it's good if you talked it up, and if you're willing to try it, I should be too."

Sophie smiled back at her. "That's the spirit!" she replied. It really was good for them to try new things every now and then after all. Sophie pulled out her phone to glance at the time. It was already nearing noon, and she realized that she actually needed to get running. While it was great that she had enjoyed her morning and her lunch, she also knew that it would be a good idea for her to get started on her work as soon as possible if she wanted to do it all that day.

She finished up her meal quickly, enjoying every last succulent bite on her plates, and went out of her way to pay for everything. As she was collecting her receipt, she heard the woman next to her ask for the octopus and smiled to herself. She was glad that her adventure had not only helped her but the woman next to her as well. It would be good for her to get that new experience out of everything.

So, with her belly full, and feeling a bit better after having done something new for the first time in a while, being unpredictable, Sophie took in a deep breath and moved out of her way to get going. She picked up her purse and hopped into her car, feeling justified, invigorated, and happier for the day. It was the perfect way to head off on her own.

Story 5: Road Trip!

Road trip!! Sophie is bored with her time at home and wants to go somewhere new. She's ready to get out on her way and see the world—or at least, whatever of the world exists along the interstate within about ten hours of their location. Join Sophie, Cara, and Felix as they head off to enjoy a quick weekend camping trip.

Beep! Beep! Beep!

The banging sound of Sophie's alarm clock made her groan to herself as she forced her eyes to open. She didn't want to be awake—but she was. It was the last thing she really wanted to be doing, but she knew that she didn't have a choice in the matter. They were set to get going for their camping trip that day, and she knew that if she didn't get going, Felix would be worried that they'd be too late to get there. They had to drive seven hours, then get themselves settled into their camping site before they did anything else. It was perfect—they'd get there, and they'd have plenty of time to unpack, set up shelter, and everything else.... And all they had to do to make it happen was get up at the ungodly hour of 2 am. She forced herself to roll herself out of bed and walked into the bathroom, blinking blearily as she tried to force her eyes to focus.

As she turned on the light, she felt her eyes burning as they struggled to adjust, and she lazily turned on the shower and began to brush her teeth. It wasn't her idea of fun—but she knew that Felix would be thrilled, and Cara was game to try it out too, even though she usually found herself happiest in luxury hotels. She was willing to make an exception for her best friend, and though Sophie wasn't quite sure what to expect as they went, she was also pretty sure that they would have a grand time doing anything that they set their mind to.

So, off she went into the shower to force herself to wake up a bit more. She knew that she'd be needing at least a few coffees before the day was over. She stepped into the shower to wake herself up, spending a few moments, enjoying the warmth as she made her way through her normal showering routine. It should be a good day, she told herself as she made her way through everything.

Before long, she was showered, dressed, and packed up, with her bag of packed goods all setup. She had plenty of dried foods that would not perish on the way, and she had a duffel bag full of her clothes next to an air mattress and a sleeping bag. Felix was bringing the rest of the stuff as far as she knew, and before long, she saw the lights flashing outside her house as

Felix pulled into her driveway. With a yawn and a mug of coffee in hand, she stepped outside, holding the door open so Felix and Koda could come inside. They walked in together, and she smiled at him, giving him a quick peck on the cheek as he did. "Hey, honey," she told him.

"Hey!" he replied, looking far more awake than she was in the moment. "You ready?"

Sophie nodded, leaning against his chest, sleepily for a moment. She was thoroughly exhausted, but she wasn't going to let that stand in her way of having a good time that day. He smelled of sandalwood and clean laundry as she rested there, and she smiled against his chest. "Thanks for stopping by," she murmured against him.

"No, thank you for coming with me," he replied with a soft smile in return, putting a hand against her head. "We're still waiting for Cara, right?"

"Mhm. She should be here soon," replied Sophie through a big yawn.

"I hope so," Felix said, looking at his watch. They had to get going, or they'd be late. "Where's your stuff?"

"In the hallway." Sophie gestured over her shoulder to where the duffel bag, sleeping bag, and mattress were waiting. "Should I load it up now?"

"I'll do it," Felix insisted, planting a kiss against her forehead. "I've got a place for everything, and—"

"Everything is in its place?" Sophie finished for him, looking up with a sleepy, smug smile.

"Exactly! You understand me," Felix bantered back, winking as he made his way to go get the bags. Koda plopped himself on the floor, next to where Bella was sleeping. Neither of them seemed too keen to be up in the middle of the night when they had better things to do—like sleeping. But, of course, they needed to get on the road sooner rather than later so they'd have time to get through their unpacking, so they had no real choice. Drastic times call for drastic measures and all that.

While Felix was busy organizing the space in the back of his big SUV, Sophie saw Cara pull in. She had someone else sitting in her Prius, but Sophie couldn't quite make out the face. It was too hard to see through the car, and she couldn't help it—she had to stare. Of course, she'd find out in a moment.

Out hopped Cara and Alyssa was with her. Sophie was pleasantly surprised, but she glanced over to Felix to see what his reaction was. He didn't seem fazed at all to be going camping with two other women, apparently, so Sophie shrugged it off. It would be fine, she was sure. She smiled widely and went up to her friends to give them a quick hug. "Hey, Alyssa! I didn't know you were coming!"

"Mmm, Cara didn't want to go on his own. She didn't want to be the third wheel, after all." She smiled, but Cara seemed to blush. Even in the darkness, it was obvious that she was flustered by what she heard, and Sophie smiled. "don't worry, Cara, there's no harm in that!" Sophie nodded in agreement.

"I'm sure it'll be fine. Besides, the more, the merrier, right?" As long as they'd all fit in Felix's car, that was.

Felix walked over to them after finishing loading up Sophie's belongings and looked at the newcomers. "Hey, Cara, Alyssa," he nodded to each of them as he went by. He was totally fine with the fact that there were more people there, as far as Sophie could tell, and that was plenty for her. She was totally happy with that result. "Where are your guys' things so I can pack them away?"

Cara pointed to her car. "In the trunk. They should fit, I hope."

"I hope so too!" Felix said with a chuckle, heading over to get the last of the things out. Before long, they had packed everything into the car, piled the dogs into the back row of his SUV, popped Cara and Alyssa into the second-row captain's chairs, and Sophie sat next to Felix in the front. It was 3:32 when he finally turned on his car, and they set off, and they had ten hours to get to where they were going.

Sophie yawned as he pulled out of the parking spot. The house was all locked up, and Cara's car was safely parked in the garage, and off they went. It was still inhumanely dark outside—no sane people were up at that hour except for them, as far as Sophie could see, but she wasn't willing to let that stop her from having fun. She looked out her window with another yawn as they started driving.

Felix's car was surprisingly comfortable in the dark, Sophie found herself thinking as they dorve. She was comfortable where she sat, looking absently out the window. It had plenty of space for all of them and everything in the trunk as well, and she was thrilled about that. It was so great to have that space in there, and Felix had even turned on some soft music. It had a soft, pulsing beat to it, somewhere between electronica and synth. It was almost like video game music, Sophie thought, but the beat was enough to keep her awake, driving them forward as the moments ticked by. Little by little, she found herself staring out the window. Little by little, she found herself getting sleepier and sleepier...

The sky was already brightening by the time that Sophie woke up with a stiff crick in her neck. It hurt as she straightened herself out, looking around. Dawn was spreading across the sky and shining brightly as she looked to the sky and a glance at the clock said that it was already 5:30. She had slept for almost two hours.

"Welcome back," Felix said with a smile, reaching over and patting her hand. "Feel better?"

Sophie nodded, rubbing at her neck. "Yeah, but my neck is killing me." She looked over her shoulder and saw that both Cara and Alyssa had also fallen asleep, but they hadn't woken up yet. She smiled at her friends as she saw them, not thinking much about what they were doing at that point. "Man, we've still got a ways to go, huh?"

Looking out her window showed that there was nothing around them—they were driving through a huge field that looked like it could go on forever—there were no endings in sight as she looked around, and she was pleasantly surprised. It was nice to see that there were no people around, but it also made the road feel kind of strangely abandoned. Living in a big city, it wasn't often that Sophie noticed that there weren't other people sharing the road. But surely, no one was stupid enough to get out of bed at 2 am on a Saturday to go driving throughout the state to the middle of nowhere. It seemed like a fool's mission, and yet there they were, heading to do exactly that.

The grass around them was yellowed and billowing in the wind, and she could see the occasional cow grazing in the distance. They were in some sort of rural land with no signs of the modern city that she lived by. It was strange just how detached they were from their surroundings or just how different things could be without much change going on in return.

They continued on their way without much to say, simply listening to the music as it played. They didn't want to wake up any of their sleeping passengers, so they chose to keep quiet instead. Instead, Sophie chose to look around at all of the random things she could find out and about around her. She saw things like cars with strange bumper stickers, strange cars, out of state license plates, and even someone driving a strangely nondescript box truck, riding around with rainbow-colored hair and a clown nose on his face. That one, she was never quite able to figure out.

Eventually, however, they made it to where they were going. The plains turned into forest, and forest turned into a mountain, which eventually flattened into even more plains. After several rests stops, stops for food and coffee, and simply getting lost a few times at strange turns, they eventually made their way all the way to their campsite.

The site was remote—not like what Sophie had in mind. She had been thinking that they would be staying in tents, but no: They were at a strange cabin that she had never seen before. Now, it was admittedly a nice cabin, but Sophie had been under the impression that they were outside.

"Okay, now that's my kind of camping!" Cara announced with a grin as she looked at the great, big cabin in front of her. It was beautifully crafted and completely surrounded by forest. There was a fire pit outside of the cabin, and a small creek that ran past it.

Alyssa looked around with wide eyes. "Where are we?" she asked. She pulled out her phone—but there was no service where they were. There would be no way for her to get a hold of anyone there. She frowned down at her phone. "And what do we do in an emergency?"

"Oh, don't worry about it," Felix said with a smile. "This is one of my parents' cabins. I camp here all the time. We have a satellite phone inside that we can use if we want to. We're pretty far out to get actual phone service here. But that's okay, the whole point was to get away for the weekend, wasn't it?"

Sophie nodded as she pulled the dogs out of the car. That was certainly the point, but now that they were there, she was feeling a bit intimidated. They were so far away from everything, and she wasn't sure what to expect.

They all walked inside and were amazed. The cabin had a massive open floorplan within it, with beautiful honey hardwood flooring and an entire wall of masonry surrounding a fireplace. There were leather sofas inside of it, with a coffee table sitting atop an ornate rug, and a massive television sat in the corner. There was an entire wall of built-in hutch along with the other, and they could see right into the kitchen as well, which was filled up with stainless steel appliances and granite counters.

There was an upstairs area as well that was where, presumably, the bedrooms were. Sophie was in awe of everything around her—but she couldn't help but wonder why they were told to pack camping stuff if they were just going to stay in a cabin. She glanced over at Felix, and he smiled at her as he let the dogs off their leashes inside of the cabin. They both happily ran into the house to go explore, and Alyssa and Cara ran upstairs into the rooms to start unpacking their belongings.

"What do you think?" asked Felix. He was watching Sophie's reaction intently as if he was genuinely curious about it. His happy smile said that he was aiming to impress, but Sophie wasn't quite sure that she'd be able to protect it. She wasn't as happy as she could have been, and she didn't know how she should tell him that.

"Well, I think that we could have a lot of fun here this weekend," said Sophie finally after searching for a tactful way to tell him exactly what she thought. She completely skirted around the issue entirely—she didn't want to tell him that his idea of camping was wrong. But, she had to admit—this was more along the lines of what she would have wanted anyway. She loved the comforts of the indoors, and sleeping on a real bed instead of an air mattress would definitely save her back—but it came at the cost of not doing what she thought they would be. No matter what, however, she knew that things would work out one way or another.

Felix's face fell. "You don't like it," he replied flatly.

"No, no, that's not it at all! It's lovely... It's just this wasn't what I had in mind when I thought we were going camping, that's all." Sophie smiled at him, reassuringly. "I'm totally happy, though. This is perfectly fine with me. I'm not sure I'd have really loved the camping anyway, to be honest."

The response seemed to confuse him further. "If this isn't camping, then what is?" asked Felix.

"You know...Tents and sleeping bags. Outside stuff, not sleeping in a private cabin." Sophie smiled. "I love the cabin, though. So, what can we do here?"

"Well, there's a hiking, hunting, fishing, ATV riding. You know, outdoorsy stuff." He looked over Sophie. "We could do whatever you wanted to. Just let me know what sounds fun."

Sophie shrugged her shoulders. "I think that right now, what I need is a nap!" she replied. It had been a long drive there, and Sophie was more than ready to tuck herself in for a bit. She wanted to stretch her back and actually find some comfort.

Felix nodded. "I'll show you the bedroom." He took her hand and guided her up the stairs and to the second floor, where there were four rooms all lined up. "Those two are the smaller guest bedrooms, and it sounds like Cara and Alyssa already took those. Then, this is a bathroom, and this is the master bedroom." He opened the door to reveal a large bedroom, with a recliner in the corner and a king-sized sleigh bed, with the frame made out of beautiful cherry wood. There were dressers against the back wall and a television mounted on the wall, connected to a DVD player. "We don't get any cable or service here, but we have a ton of DVDs if you want a movie night."

Sophie looked around in awe. The room was beautiful. There were some nice floral paintings on the wall, and the big, bay window in the bedroom was stunning. She looked at it all and nodded her head. "Looks great."

"The bathroom is over there, too," he said, pointing to the bathroom that was connected to the bedroom. "There's a big soaking tub in there that you can use if you want to." Felix dropped off their bags inside the room. "I'll leave you to it, honey," he said with one last kiss on her head. "I've got some stuff to set up to make sure that we're good for the entire weekend, but I'll come up here to join you later, okay?"

Sophie nodded her head as she pulled off her shoes. She was too tired to protest, or even change out of her jeans that she had worn in the car. She climbed into bed and was immediately greeted by the softest, plushest mattress surface she had ever felt, and she was in *love*.

It barely took any time at all for her to fall asleep, wrapped up in a comfortable blanket. In fact, she was probably asleep before her head even hit the pillow. After all, long car rides like that were utterly exhausting, and she was ready to rest.

Story 6: Happy Birthday!

It's Cara's birthday!! Sophie is thrilled that her best friend is another year older and she is so ready to party! But, she must get everything set up, so her friend doesn't realize that everyone is gathering for a surprise birthday party. Wish Sophie luck as she does her best to remain unspotted as she sets everything up once and for all. Can she fly under the radar long enough to surprise Cara? Only time will tell!

It was a special day. Not just because it was the second Friday of the month, or because Sophie's favorite sushi restaurant was giving off food for 50% off. No, that day was special because it was Cara's birthday, and Sophie was determined to make it as special as possible. She was ready to ensure that everything that Cara did was exciting, pleasing, and would leave Cara feeling loved and appreciated. After all, Cara was such a sweetheart—she deserved a good party!

Of course, that meant that Sophie needed to figure out how to outdo the parties that she was certain that Cara's family would throw for her. But, Sophie had the condolence of knowing that Cara disliked the fanfare and crazy efforts that would go into a big party. Cara wanted smaller, intimate gatherings with her closest friends—not parties that forced her to kindly go around and say hello to every single person she passed. Sophie wanted Cara to enjoy her party, not walk around like another prop that had to introduce herself to everyone. After all, what fun was it when you had to thank everyone for coming to a party that you didn't want to be in the first place?

Sophie looked down at her phone. She had a few messages from her friends saying that they would be there at the party. All they had to do was show up. All they had to do was figure out how they were going to hide everything from Cara.

Speaking of Cara, Sophie heard her phone start to go off and glancing at it, she could see that it was Cara who was calling her right that moment. Sophie's eyes widened, and she gasped a little bit, feeling that sudden shock—that concern that she had to make sure that she wasn't spotted. She had to make sure that she wasn't going to be found out somehow. So, Sophie answered the phone and put on her best fake happy voice. "Hey, Cara! What's up?" She was trying her hardest to pretend that everything was normal.

"Oh, nothing," Cara replied. "I was just wondering if you wanted to go out for lunch today. My treat!" Sophie could hear that her voice sounded unconvinced—she wasn't fully confident that Sophie would agree, and Sophie felt a pang of guilt. She'd have to lie to get out of it, or she wouldn't be able to finish up the birthday party.

"Oh, Cara," she said, using her best disappointed voice. "I'm so sorry! I've actually got a uh... Gynecologist appointment this afternoon." She chose out the most invasive routine appointment she could think of—and what would be more invasive than a pap smear? Hopefully, Cara wouldn't ask any more questions after that, she told herself as she looked over her shoulder to look at the time.

"Oh, dear..." Cara replied, sounding mildly concerned. "I'm sorry to hear that! But, thanks anyway. Maybe we can try for dinner?" Her voice sounded a bit more hopeful then.

"I'll try, but no promises... I've got some crazy deadlines I have to meet today," Sophie answered. "I'm sorry, honey. I don't like having to tell you no. Why? Is today special?"

Cara hesitated for a moment. "No, not at all. Good luck at your appointment and thanks anyway! Love you, talk to you soon!" And with that said, she hung up the phone.

Sophie sighed, putting her phone onto the table. She felt incredibly guilty telling Cara no, especially on her birthday, but hopefully, it would all be worth it by the time that they were done. She had high hopes that things would be perfect—they just needed the time to get through everything. Sophie was tasked with decorating her home while Alyssa picked up the birthday cake, and Felix said he would pick up some catering on his way. They should be able to get everything just right and hopefully would all be ready at exactly 1:30. That would give her plenty of time to contact Cara and tell her to hurry over as quickly as she could, and Sophie was hoping that she wouldn't feel too rejected and just skip when she called.

So, Sophie got to work, trying her best to get everything as organized as she could to ensure that everything looked perfect. She was wiping down counters and polishing the cabinets. When everything was clean, she moved on to decorations. All sorts of them went up around her—she put up balloons first, blowing them up on her own. They had chosen mint green and silver balloons for her birthday party decorations—colors that Sophie knew that Cara would love. She blew up at least a few dozen of each by herself, blowing directly into them so she could hang them up on the walls and counter corners. They were draped down from some streamers and attached to the ceiling in some places, too.

Another couple dozen balloons were blown up with a helium tank Sophie had picked up at the store, tying them up with matching ribbons and then securing them in clusters of three or four in various areas. There were a few in the center of the table, weighed down with a big, silver weight with streamers and tinsel coming out of it. It was just gaudy enough that Sophie was sure that Cara would love it. After all, Cara was one of those people who loved to do things backward from what her family expected of her. Though her family was incredibly wealthy, she wanted nothing to do with the idea that she was better than other people. No—Cara would be willing to give a gift, or even the very shirt off of her back if she needed to. She was totally happy doing things that the upper class might scoff at, such as going to theaters to watch a movie or going camping. Yeah, Sophie had to admit that her idea of average life was a bit out of touch sometimes, but Cara was such a good friend that she deserved to be showered with lavish attention. If anyone deserved to have that kind of wealth, Sophie often told herself, it was Cara thanks to her attitude.

Before long, Sophie had finished up all of the balloons, and it was time to start on with the streamers that she had bought. They had to be carefully twisted around each other before they were hung up so they would nicely combine. Sophie wasn't quite sure what she was doing, but she had seen it once on Pinterest and figured she could do it herself. Of course, Sophie also refused to admit the existence of the dreaded Pinterest fails as well... Which is exactly what he streamers eventually became.

Sophie frowned, looking at her tangle of tissue streamers, and shook her head with a sigh. It was harder than it looked. Again, her phone went off, and when she checked it, she saw a message from Alyssa. She was warning Sophie that Cara was asked to hang out that afternoon and that Cara never said a word about her birthday either. Sophie felt her brows furrow, and she shook her head. She had to hurry up before Cara got too impatient and just came over!

Instead of trying to add some pizzazz to the streamers, Sophie changed tactic—she just hung them up the normal way without trying to figure out how to put them up in any sort of fancy manner. It wouldn't matter, would it? There was no way it could matter that much; she told herself and simply shifted her efforts. Streamers went up. Balloons were blown and hung around. And, Sophie told herself that things were looking great.

Next, Alyssa arrived, carrying a box of cake. The box was quickly placed on the counter. "Can I do anything to help?" asked Alyssa kindly. She smiled up at her friend.

"You know, you could help me figure out how to put these streamers up. I'm really not doing a very good job!" Sophie smiled sheepishly. "Sorry," she told her friend.

"No, it looks fine over there! But I'm happy to help. No need to apologize! Just gotta get to work!" Alyssa happily began to put everything up and where it belonged. She was ready to take care of it all. "How about you get all of the space ready for the food while I do this?"

That sounded perfect. "You are a godsend, Alyssa; you know that?" Sophie told her friend with a relieved grin. "Thank you!!" So, off Sophie went, getting the tablecloth all set up and then lining everything up. Felix was bringing back a bunch of appetizers for them all to enjoy with some wine, so Sophie had a bit of an organization to do. She double-checked that the bottles of wine were in the fridge, that she knew where the bottle opener was, and she set up ten wine glasses that they could use to give everyone their drinks. It was perfect! They just had to wait for the food to get there.

And, as if on cue, in came Felix, holding several

baking sheet half pans of food. They were all stacked upon each other carefully, with three piled together. "There's more in the car, hon, can you get them?"

Sophie nodded and ran out, gathering up some more of the boxes. She was eager to get them all to put away as soon as possible. The clock was ticking, and they'd need to hurry up if they wanted to do everything the right way!

They carefully unloaded all of the food, carefully keeping it in the foil to keep it warm. "Are you ready for me to call her over?" Sophie looked at the clock. Everyone else should be piling in within the next few minutes, and Cara lived twenty minutes away, so calling then seemed like a fair bet.

Alyssa nodded her agreement. "Yeah, good idea!" she told her as she looked to Felix, who simply shrugged his shoulder, munching on a carrot stick from one of the trays.

"Hey! Leave it for later!" Sophie told him playfully with a quick swat on the hand. "You shouldn't be eating that!"

"Sorry, sorry! It was my delivery fee!" Felix added quickly with a chuckle as Sophie dialed in Cara's number.

The phone barely rang before Cara answered. "Hey, what's up? Are you okay? How did your appointment with the lady doctor go?" Cara was talking a mile a minute—she was upset. Sophie could tell instantly. She felt forgotten.

"Oh, you know, I wanted to talk to you about that. Can you come over right now? I really need to see you." Sophie glanced over to the door, seeing out the window that there were a few more people walking up. They were all told to park down the street from Sophie's house so they wouldn't have their car give away the party.

"Yeah, I can do that. I'll be there in twenty." Cara sounded curious, but she didn't pry any deeper.

"Thanks, honey!" Sophie said. "See you soon!" She hung up the phone and glanced at their friends. It was time to get situated. "Okay, guys, she's on her way now. We're going to have to be careful if we want to surprise her. Where can we hide…?"

"Couldn't we just turn off all the lights and curtains and scream 'Surprise!!' when she walked in?" asked Felix. He had a point, too. Wasn't that what they normally did with surprise parties? Wasn't that how they always did it in the movies?

"Perfect. We've got a few minutes, and everyone else is on their way… This might actually work!" Sophie grinned at her friends.

"Good job, team! Let's make this happen!" Sophie looked at her friends, who looked back at her with their own smiles in return.

"Will Cara like this?" asked Felix, looking around at the party. He was more than happy to help, but it seemed like something that she wouldn't necessarily care for.

Sophie nodded in return. "This is exactly what she needs," she replied. "She loves the simpler things in life, and this is right up her alley. She loves silly birthday parties. I remember that one year, she told me that she wished her family had done surprise parties. They always did weird gala things, and she's pretty done with them.

Felix nodded his head. "Yeah, the birthday galas aren't exactly all that fun…" he said as he trailed off, losing himself in his thoughts. Clearly, he was somewhere else, and Sophie wasn't about to interrupt him. As the last-minute stragglers started to arrive, Sophie worried that she had not actually done enough. She worried that Cara would not actually like what she had arranged. What if she hated the colors? Or the balloons?

Sophie's face betrayed her stress. Everyone around her could see it clear as day in her eyes. "You know, I bet she'll love it," said Felix with a quick nod of his head. He was totally convinced that this was exactly what she needed after hearing what Sophie had to say. "She'll be thrilled that you did all of this for her when she is used to all those galas. You've got this!"

Sophie smiled at him. "I sure hope you're right," she replied.

And, she couldn't dwell any longer—she saw Cara's Prius pull into the driveway. She knew that Cara would just walk right in—they didn't knock at each other's homes. "Quick, everyone, get in place!!"

Everyone ducked to hide somewhere that they could. Behind the bar—behind walls and more. And, as soon as Cara opened the door, she was greeted with a loud cry of "SURPRISE!!" from everyone in the room.

Cara stopped and stared in shock. She had not been expecting that at all—and now, there was everyone, standing in her way, staring at her. They were all watching her and waiting for her reaction. Her purse fell out of her hand and onto the floor. She looked from person to person in the group, and her eyes trailed all around the room, absorbing in the decorations and watching closely. She seemed entirely surprised to see the party there—she hadn't been expecting it, but that was exactly the point as far as Sophie was concerned.

"For me?" Cara asked, looking around. Her voice wavered. She looked like she was fighting back the tears, and Sophie felt guilty. She didn't want to make her friend cry—that had been an accident! She hadn't meant to make her friend lose it.

"For you," Sophie confirmed, looking closely for any sign of happiness. But, Cara's tears came almost immediately, and Sophie ran to her. "What's wrong? I thought you've always wanted a surprise birthday party?" She gazed deeply into Cara's eyes, looking for any sign of an answer.

"Yes, I have always wanted one of these... that's why I'm crying." She smiled at Sophie tearfully. "I'm sorry! I don't want to bring down the mood. I can see that you worked really hard on everything that is here, and I don't want it to go to waste. It's really beautiful, Sophie. You've really outdone yourself here!" She sniffled a bit and looked at everyone else there as well. "Thank you all. I'm so glad you all came out here today and that you all came over to support me. It's so sweet of you all to be here, and I cannot thank you enough for your love and kindness you've shown to me." She looked at everyone again. "You know, my family wanted me to sit at some sort of dinner to bring everyone together, but they don't throw parties. We all just sit, eat some food, make some small talk, and move on with our lives as nothing has happened. I'm sick of it... But you all? You're like family... And thank you." Cara was tearing up again, and Sophie smiled sympathetically.

"Thanks for coming so quickly when I called you, too," Sophie told her in return. "I know that I can count on you when I need you, and I wanted to give you that happiness in return. I wanted you to know that wherever you are and whatever you do, you can count on me to be there too! I want you to know that you can trust me to help you and to bring you that happiness and love in your life when you need it the most. Thanks for being such a good friend, Cara. You deserve the world!"

Felix clapped his hands, and as he did, everyone else started to clap as well. "Enough of the friendship mumbo jumbo... Let's all dig in! I'm starving!"

Everyone laughed at Felix as he said this. He started opening up all of the appetizer dishes that he had brought with him, and he lined up all of them for everyone to get their fill. Everyone started talking and enjoying themselves, getting plates of food and glasses of wine, and they all smiled at Cara, wishing her a happy birthday.

Sophie smiled and patted her friend on the back. "I'm glad you love your party," she told Cara. "I was terrified you'd hate it!"

"Hate it? Why?" Cara looked genuinely surprised—she hadn't expected that.

"I don't know...Maybe because it isn't very fancy or something. I've tried, though, and I wanted you to feel that love and appreciation the way that I do when I'm with you!" Sophie plopped her head on Cara's shoulder. "Happy birthday, friend."

"Thank you, Sophie," Cara replied, leaning her own head onto Sophie's. They sat there for a few moments.

"You know this means you're old now, right?" Sophie said after a few moments of silence.

Cara feigned offense. "Old? Me? Never!!" she cried back, shaking her head. "No, no, no. You've got me mixed up. I'm still young! See? No greys!"

They both laughed. Being that close to a best friend was always a perk, and she was thrilled to have her own best friend always around.

The party was a success. The food was enjoyed, all three bottles of wine were happily drunk, and the cake... Was less than perfect, but tasted delicious! The orders had accidentally been swapped, and by mistake, they wound up with a kid's birthday cake, with some superhero dogs riding in vehicles on it, but it tasted fantastic. The chocolate with strawberry filling really brought the night together, Sophie thought as she grinned, looking at her friends and family around her. It was a perfect day as far as she was concerned—she just had to trust that Car enjoyed her day too.

Story 7: Novel Heights

Sophie has always been terrified of heights. Going up mountains and looking over them? Terrifying. Going over bridges? Nerve-wracking! She hates going over cliffs or looking out the windows when she was up on the higher floors. So, when Cara begs her to go up to the Space Needle in Seattle, she's faced with two options: Turn it down because she can't handle the height, or go up anyway and force herself to face her fears. Join Sophie as she tries her hardest to head up and ends up enjoying the views, realizing that the heights aren't actually as bad as she thought and that they can actually be appreciated!

"Okay, I'll see you at 4:30!" Sophie announced with a falsetto in her voice. She tried to sound excited for her friend on the phone as she hung up, looking down. She could see the picture of Cara from her social media account staring back up at her, and Sophie sighed. "Don't give me that look!" she demanded huffily as she stared at her friend's profile picture. "You know I hate heights, lady!" She shook her head and looked out the window. Surely, there was a way they could get out of going up to the Space Needle in Seattle. Surely, they'd be able to get out of having to ride that big, see-through elevator as they were taken up nearly 500 feet to the top. Surely she could get by without having to see the city from such a high view. Sure, some people loved it, but Sophie? Nope.

Keep her away from anything even remotely resembling heights—she hated them all. It was one of those things from childhood that she never outgrew after she fell off a bunk bed in elementary school and broke her arm. Ever since the idea of heights defined loosely as anything more than maybe four feet off the ground was appalling.

Sure, her room was on the second floor of a house. Sure, she had to climb the stairs every night. But, that didn't mean that she had to look down the stairs or even out her window regularly. She could live in utter denial of her fear of heights without repercussions most of the time. Of course, Cara was there to completely and utterly demolish that idea. Of *course,* Cara would choose the one thing that would instill fear into Sophie without meaning to, and of *course*, Sophie would feel compelled to follow through with it anyway. Sophie had no real recourse. She had no real way to tell her friend no when there wasn't a reasonable reason to say no in the first place. She had no choice—she would have to go or tell her friend the truth.

"Just suck it up, Sophie," she told herself. Bella looked up at her, confused, but Sophie didn't budge. "You can do this. The heights aren't that scary, and the elevator isn't going to fail on you. You're not going to fall. You don't even have to look down at the ground. You can look up at the sky instead. Or, you can look at Cara, or at your reflection, or even close your eyes... You can do this. You don't have to be so worried!" Just suck it up and make it happen so you can be happy. You've got this!!" Sophie, despite her pep-talking, wasn't convinced, however. She was certain that she was going to be utterly miserable, cry at some point, and maybe even completely embarrass herself somehow. She wasn't convinced that she could keep it together long enough to get to the top of the Space Needle and actually look at the whole city of Seattle without fear. She was too terrified to do that. She was horrified.

The what-ifs raced through her mind. What if there was an earthquake while they were going there? What if there was lightning striking it? What if there was a problem with the elevator? What if all of the people on the elevator were too heavy to get it up to the top? What if the attendant had a death wish and decided to open up the door somehow halfway up so the wind could blow them out? What if the whole building collapsed? Or if there was a fire? She shook her head back and forth, desperately trying to clear her mind.

Of course, the Space Needle would be a safe place to go—it was designed the way that it was for a reason. It was designed to be safe and durable. It was meant to be somewhere that they would be able to stay safe and to be somewhere that they'd be able to enjoy. It was meant to withstand earthquakes and the wind because that is something that happened regularly in the area. While massive earthquakes weren't unheard of, they weren't common, and the building had managed to survive through many different windstorms. It couldn't be that bad if it could do all of that, right? It couldn't be something impossible to rely on if it was capable of being so dependable and reliable? It couldn't possibly be doomed for failure if thousands of people daily go through it.

Sophie sighed. She took in a deep breath. "Get a grip, Sophie," she told herself. "You're letting your stress get the best of you again." She breathed in... And out... And she tried her hardest to relax a bit more. There was no reason to be so terrified, she reminded herself. It would be fun, she insisted. She didn't have to be so afraid, she told herself, and she took another deep breath. They didn't live in Seattle, but they were near it. She knew that they'd have to get over there sooner rather than later, and she was sure she'd find a way to get over it.

They were going for an evening viewing of the Space Needle in hopes of seeing the sunset and the nighttime view. Sure, it was bound to be beautiful, but it was also going to be intimidating as far as Sophie was concerned. After all, they'd still be high up.

4:30 came quicker than Sophie had hoped, and soon, they were hopped into Cara's car and on their way to Seattle. They lived about an hour south of the Emerald City, and it was a straight shot to get there on the interstate. Off they went, with Cara happily babbling about everything that they were going to do, see, and enjoy. She was thrilled to get the opportunity and Sophie... Was hesitant. She wasn't quite convinced this was what she wanted, but she was accepting that it was what they were doing. All she had to do was smile and nod... Smile and nod...

"You know what I'm looking forward to, though?" asked Cara with a grin, glancing at her friend in the driver's seat.

"What?" asked Sophie, feeling her stomach drop. She had a feeling that she was not going to like the answer that she got. "The glass floors. Can you believe it? Glass *floors!!*"

That sounded absolutely terrifying. Not fun at all. Nope—all of the alarm bells were ringing in Sophie's mind. Avoiding looking down on the glass elevator was one thing, but having to avoid looking down the entire time? What if she had to look at her phone? Or go tie her shoe? Or dig her wallet out of her purse? There were a million little reasons she would have to look at her phone with all of them being reasonable, and yet doing so would be horrifying. She wasn't sure how well she could cope with that, to be frank, but she knew she had to try.

"Sophie?" Cara called out, trying to snap Sophie out of her stress-induced reverie. "What's up? You seem distracted."

Sophie shook her head. "No, no, it's nothing! I'm fine!" She smiled. "I just need a coffee, that's all."

Cara looked unconvinced. "If you say so…" She replied, quirking a perfectly sculpted brow at her friend. "Well, you know what they say. There's plenty of coffee in Seattle!" They were almost there at that point—they had maybe another twenty minutes to go before they'd be parked—assuming they found parking, which in Seattle, was a hot commodity. "I heard there's a café in the Space Needle, too, so you can pick up a coffee as soon as we get there. How's that sound?"

"Perfect!" Sophie announced with another fake smile, turning to look out the window again. She was running out of time to build up her resolve enough to get up to the Space Needle, and she had no idea how she would do so or how she could possibly get out of this predicament that she had somehow gotten herself tangled up in. She was stuck. Stucker than stuck—she had no choice but to just *do it*.

And, before she knew it, she had no other choice. They were standing in front of the Space Needle, and she looked up. It was so tall that, from the bottom, she had to crane her neck all the way back to see it. The line was mostly filled with college students wearing purple sweatshirts with the letters *UW* emblazoned across them, courtesy of the local state university, and they all looked thrilled to be there. They were all chatting excitedly, and Sophie watched them all, baby-faced, happily get into the elevator without a single complaint, and here Sophie was, whining about how scared she was.

"... Sophie?"

Sophie blinked her eyes and turned to look at Cara. She looked concerned, and Sophie wasn't sure why.

"You're not doing okay, are you?" Cara looked over Sophie once more.

"I'm fine. Why?"

"No, you're not. You're shaking, and I don't understand why you keep lying to me," Cara replied. She shook her head with a sigh. "You don't have to hide things from me, you know."

"I know, I... Honestly? It's embarrassing." Sophie looked at the next group of people, watching as they all piled into the elevator without a single hesitation. "I'm afraid of heights."

Cara stared at her in disbelief. "Afraid of heights?"

"Yup."

"How?" Cara seemed shocked at the idea. "I mean... I thought the Acropolis was your favorite thing we saw in Greece, and that was so high up." She frowned as they moved up in line. "Do you want to head home?"

"It was my favorite! I... Just don't do well with heights. They scare me. But I loved being there. It was a childhood dream of mine, and so that kinda helped me get over the fear, I guess? But, I was terrified, in a good way." Sophie trailed off, looking around. "No, I don't want to leave, but uh... Could I maybe hold your hand when we go up?" She looked up at Cara, almost embarrassed that she had even asked.

Cara smiled. "Of course," she said. And, before she could say another word, they were ushered into the elevator for their own turn. "As soon as that door closes, you're stuck, you know," she reiterated to Sophie, who nodded.

Sophie was well aware of what she was getting herself into, and for Cara, she was happy to do so. She just had to suck it up and make it happen. She just had to close her eyes, hold Cara's hand, and pretend that they were at home like nothing was happening...

Cara reached out to take Sophie's hand and gave her a reassuring squeeze as the doors closed. Then, the elevator began moving up, little by little. It made its way up, floor by floor, and the ground underneath them vanished. Sophie squeezed Cara's hand back and tried her hardest to stare up at the sky instead. It was an uncharacteristically clear day for a Seattle autumn evening. The sky was a perfect shade of blue, connecting in the distance to the hilly horizon. She watched a few birds fly by, as the crowd around her exclaimed their own awe at what they were doing. The entire elevator ride wasn't terrible, but Sophie had also refused to look down at that point. She could feel her heart pounding away in her chest. She was terrified at what she might see if she looked at the ground as it disappeared.

Breathe... Just breathe... In... And out... In... And out...

Sophie tried her hardest to just focus on her breath, but it was hard for her. It was hard for her to act like there wasn't a single problem as she made her way up the needle. But, holding Cara's hand helped a lot. Being there with her friend, who knew that she was afraid and was willing to comfort her, meant a lot to her, and she was glad that she was lucky enough to have that courtesy.

The elevator stopped, and they were all ushered into the building. There was plenty to see there, and thankfully, not the entire floor was glass. There were parts of the floor that were solid as well, and Sophie did her best to focus on those. But, it was impossible for her to avoid looking out at the heights—the entire building was one long, windowed corridor. Everything was windowed—the walls were made of massive panels of glass, and the flooring was also glass across much of it. It was strange being so high up, and she had no idea how to really feel about it. She was up that high, but as she looked out, she realized it wasn't so bad. It was more like looking at a postcard scene.

She stopped and looked out the window. She could see a big cluster of skyscrapers that made up much of downtown Seattle, and directly to the right, she could see a massive body of water, with treed land in the far distance on the other side. It was strange being that high up—but it was also beautiful. The sun was very rapidly setting, too, and the sky was starting to tinge with pinks and oranges.

"Sophie?"

Cara's voice shocked her out of her reverie, and Sophie turned to look at her. "Hmm?"

"Are you doing okay?" Cara looked concerned, watching her friend closely. She had a look that almost said that she thought that Sophie would explode if they weren't careful, and that wasn't okay with her. Her own feelings were her own to manage—not Cara's.

Sophie nodded her head. "You know, this view is actually pretty great, as long as I don't look down at the ground." Sophie chuckled. "You know, it's a beautiful view, and I have to admit—it is something that I would never have done on my own. I'm glad you convinced me to go."

"Convinced you? I just asked you!" Cara looked at her with surprise. "You didn't sound like you were terrified of heights when I asked you to go. You sounded excited. Why?" Cara watched her closely, waiting to see if she would lie about anything.

"Oh, well, you know, I just wanted to be a good friend. I wanted to support you in what you were doing and what you wanted to do, and if that meant that I had to go up this giant building, even if I'm afraid, I wanted to be there with you. And you know what the weird thing is? I'm not so afraid any more—I'm not so terrified because you're here with me, and that makes all the difference. How could I possibly be afraid of such a good friend right here with me? What could I possibly have to be afraid of if you are here right by my side? This is because of you." Sophie smiled softly and squeezed her friend's hand. "You've always made me a better person, Cara, and I can't tell you how much I appreciate it."

Cara's cheeks tinged red in embarrassment. "No way, Soph. This is your victory. Don't try pinning it on me this time! Just own it—accept that you're a great person, and let's move on. We can do that, right?" Cara laughed, and so did Sophie.

"Well, it wouldn't hurt to watch the view. The sun's setting now—isn't it supposed to be stunning up here in the nighttime?" Sophie grinned at Cara. She had seen the postcards before—the picture of the buildings all lit up nicely, and the city streets all brightly lit with cars. It was a gorgeous sight to behold, and she was honestly looking forward to it now that she had gotten past that bit of fear. It would be better than she had imagined as far as she could tell, and she was ready for it.

So, together, Sophie and Cara sat at one of the benches of the Space Needle, enjoying the sights as the entire building slowly and lazily rotated. Their view of the surrounding area was constantly shifting with the moving floor, and though it was a bit strange at first, Sophie also found it strangely comforting. It was nice to know that she didn't have to walk across the surface of the glass, and it would move for her to get a full panoramic view of everything.

One by one, the lights came on, and as the sky continued to darken, Sophie realized that her fears were entirely unfounded. She hadn't needed to be afraid at all, and honestly, from being up there, she was happier. She was enjoying the view enough to even consider going back again in the future. So, Sophie and Cara chatted together, waiting for the sky to completely darken as they watched the city lights around them. When the lights finally did turn off all the way, it was amazing to see the city in the dark. The streets were illuminated to glow almost golden colors, and the sparkling lights from the city looked like millions of stars all over the city. It was gorgeous, and there was no other word to describe it. It was a fantastic view, and she was thrilled she didn't have to miss it.

As they were heading out of the Space Needle, Sophie squeezed Cara's hand. "Thank you. I mean it."

"Don't mention it," Cara said. "Thanks for coming with me. That view was stellar!"

"It was!" replied Sophie. "We'll have to come back again sometime in the future. I'd love to see it again!"

Cara laughed. "Really? You'd be willing to come back there? Did I cure your fear of height?"

Sophie laughed back as they walked to Cara's car. "Something like that. But hey, it worked! We should do it again in the future, okay? It'll be my treat next time."

"Oh, in that case, of course! We'll have to go again. Maybe we can check out that new restaurant that they have in there... Did you know there's a revolving restaurant up there?

Isn't that cool?" Cara unlocked their car and headed inside with a grin as she started it up.

"Oh, is there?" Sophie replied as she jumped in as well. "We'll definitely have to check it out then!"

They both grinned at each other and made their way home, happily chatting about all of their adventure that day. It had been a busy one, but it was one that Sophie would love to repeat again in the future.

Guided Meditation 1: Exploring Time and Space

In this guided meditation, you will be encouraged to explore the world and the universe around you, discovering that while you may think that something is big and unbearable in the moment, you can let it go and let it fade away with ease if you simply distance yourself away from it. Even the biggest problems will not seem so bad in the grand scheme of things if you are able to take a new perspective, one that is far from the perspective that you have taken. Through traveling through space and time, you will put yourself in a position where even galaxies can seem so far away that they are insignificantly small. You learn to focus on your acceptance of the situation at hand so you can prevent yourself from letting your stress from overwhelming you. As you do this, you become able to envision your home, your room, and your bed as your safe space, distanced away from all of the stressors and anxieties of the day so you can get a restful, quiet sleep.

Close your eyes and take in a big, deep breath. Feel the air flowing through your nose. Notice how it feels. Focus in the temperature and the smells. Feel it filling up your lungs, with your lungs swelling up within you like great, big balloons in your chest until you feel like they can't swell up any more. Feel the air warming in your chest and exhale slowly, feeling the air pass your lips gently and slowly. Is it warm? With each breath that you take, you feel yourself calming down.

You breathe in... And out...

Now, feel yourself. Focus on your center, the point just above your belly button. How does it feel? Is it tense? Tight? Stressed? Focus on this point as you inhale in. One... Two... Three... Four... Five... and out... One... Two... three... Four... Five... Focus on that spot for another breath or two...

Now, feel the tension in your body. Become aware of any tension you are holding in your head and face. As you breathe in, imagine that you are pushing the tension down to the center above your belly button. Let it gather there. Now, feel the tension in your shoulders. Focus on that stress and tension and as you breathe in, feel it moving down to your center. Let it gather there, imagining your tension and stress all becoming balled up in the center. Feel the tension in your arms and hands gathering and flowing in to your center. Feel that center growing with the tension and allow it to build up. Then, take the tension from your chest and upper back, and flow it down toward your center.

Then, go down to your toes and feet, identifying the tension that is there. Push it up, feeling it flowing up your legs, through your pelvis and belly, and noting it as it arrives in the belly. Focus on it as it grows within you and allow it to flow.

Feel all of the tension in your body and imagine it turning into a flame within you. Imagine it flickering and burning within your belly, but as it burns, it is released into the world. You burn the tension more and more, helping it to release itself out of you. You reject the tension that was within you and push it to your inner core so you can allow it all to dissipate. You want to be relaxed and with every moment of burning within yourself, you find yourself relaxing more and more. Your head starts to relax and you feel your stress fading away. Your shoulders and your arms begin to relax and the fire in your belly comfortably burns it away. Your tension in your chest fades and you feel incredibly warm and comfortable. Finally, the tension from the other side begins to burn off as well, leaving your entire body entirely at ease and completely relaxed. You have released all of your tension and are left with a small, bright flame in your stomach, flickering along with your heart. With every beat, it crackles within you, helping you to stay relaxed.

With every exhale, you breathe out what was left of your tension. It gathers in your lungs with your used air. It all gathers up into one place for simple burning and you will be able to help yourself to stay relaxed. You can draw on this flame whenever you find yourself stressed with tension. Whenever you feel the need to alleviate the stress within you, you can focus on the tension and burn it within yourself, imagining as it all toasts up and burns away.

You now have space within yourself to welcome relaxation and positivity.

Breathe in... One... Two... Three... Four... Five... And out... One... Two... Three... Four... Five... As you breathe in, imagine the feeling of relaxation flowing within you, emanating from your inner fire throughout your body. Feel it in your head. Breathe in... and out... Feel the relaxation pulsating in your shoulders and arms... Feel it spreading throughout your chest. Feel it spread down to your legs and feet. It fills your whole body, bringing you utter peace and relaxation. Your mind feels incredibly open and ready to go on a peaceful, relaxing adventure. Your body is ready to fall deeper and deeper into your relaxation so you can become more and more relaxed. Your body embraces the relaxation and does not resist. It is happy to enjoy the warmth and peace within itself. It is ready to be taken on a journey.

As you become as relaxed as you can be, you are able to stop and focus on the world within you. You reflect inwardly, sinking into your mind and relax. You pull yourself into your mind, feeling more and more at peace as you do. You are ready.

You are but a speck in a field of blackness. You are surrounded by nothingness, so vast that you cannot comprehend just how wide it is. You are a drifter, but a speck in the world. You are a single point in the vastness of eternity around you. You are surrounded by everything and nothing all at the same time. As you focus around yourself, you realize that you are actually floating, unable to feel anything above or below you. You cannot feel anything touching you at all, and you can only see darkness about you. You are drifting aimlessly in the wide expanse of nothing. You cannot see anything but darkness. You do not hear anything but silence. But, you are at peace. You know that you are right where you are supposed to be. You are a single little speck, floating...

You float further and further away from your starting point without resistance. You don't know how or why you are drifting, but you are willing to accept it. You are willing to be that little speck, carried by forces that you are unsure of. You are willing to be a part of that, of being carried about, and you are content in your place. Every breath that you take pulls you further away. Every moment you end up drifting more and more, but it doesn't matter because there is nowhere to go.

You take a deep breath in...

One... Two... Three... Four... Five...

And out...

One... Two... Three... Four... Five...

As you do this, you feel yourself relaxing. You feel that little spark inside of you start to light up. It flickers into existence. Now, you are just a little bit bigger. You look around and you are surrounded by lots of tiny little specks. You can't see much—they are just little dots in the space around you, floating and drifting just as aimlessly as you are. Sometimes, they bump into you, but it doesn't matter to you. You just keep on moving within space.

You take a deep breath in...

One... Two... Three... Four... Five...

And out...

One... Two... Three... Four... Five...

You relax a little bit more. You surrender yourself to the feeling of being utterly at peace within yourself. You feel perfectly content as you float aimlessly. You grow a little bit bigger than you were before and you realize something. You are now able to do a little bit more. Now, you can move around yourself a little bit. You can sort of will yourself wherever you want and you slowly find yourself gravitating in that direction. It is incredibly freeing and you love every moment of it. You find yourself drifting about aimlessly at first, and then you start to experiment. You can move up... and you can move down... and to the sides...

You notice that you can stop running into all of the little particles floating around you... and many of them look different. There are smaller particles around you now, and some that are much larger than you, too. You realize that you're simply drifting among the particles in this great, big, vast nothingness, and you *accept it*. You are calm. You are not hurting. You are able to relax. Soon, you start moving more. You move quicker, easier. You grow larger. And as you grow, you realize something. You are floating through space and you are finally large enough to make it out.

You can see endless darkness, and the particles have disappeared around you. You are able to see stars all around you. You see something in the distance—a nebulous haze, filled with the vaguest hints of colors within them. You can see it, a sort of amalgamation of purples and blues. It all circulated around a central point. The one point in the center is entirely bright— you can't seem to make it out, but around it, the haze reaches outward, tendrils of the hazy galaxy stretching out across space. It looks so small from where you are standing... So distant, and yet you know that it is far vaster than anything you could imagine—so big, in fact, that it houses whole solar systems.

You take in a deep breath and you feel yourself moving away from the great, big galaxy. You are not ready to approach it yet. You are not yet ready to see just how vast and expansive it is. You move away from the galaxy, and see another one in the distance, and another one and another one. There are galaxies spread throughout space, some of them looking like tiny dots, barely visible while others appear much larger, with a glowing mass surrounded by spinning haze just like the last one.

All of the galaxies around you are beautiful, shimmering, and mysterious. You feel drawn to them, but you cannot help it—you want to stay back. You don't want to approach them yet. And yet, as you try to stay away, you find yourself naturally gravitating toward one. As soon as you see it, you are in awe with how beautiful it is. There is a single light point in its center, golden in color, and it stretches outward, as if several arms of nebulous haze reached out from one central point, spiraling around it. You are looking at the Milky Way galaxy. From your perspective, it swirls around that central glowing point. It wraps around, almost like a shell, and it sparkles. Each of the arms of the spiral is full of so many stars. You see them all in front of you, but you have no way to count them. You get closer and closer over time, breathing in and out as you go closer.

You breathe in…

One… Two… Three… Four…

And out…

One… Two… Three… Four…

As you continue breathing, the arms of the spiral get bigger and bigger… They get more and more white. You see that they are full of stars and spots around the stars. They are planets, rotating around the sun, more and more. They look so small as you view them. You see the planets rotating around the stars and the moons around the planets. They move faster and faster, and you can see them rotating as you breathe. The galaxy spins around that central light, all of the arms spinning. Within the arms, you can see that each one is made up of many different solar systems, each one rotating around a star. Each solar system is filled up with planets, with moons, with asteroids and more. Each one is bright and unique in its own ways. And all of them are connected together.

You breathe in…

One… Two… Three… Four…

And out...

One... Two... Three... Four...

You choose to approach one of the solar systems. The solar system's star is not very big compared to the rest. It still shines rightly right where it is, yellow-orange. Around it there are eight planets, all rotating around. You move closer through the stars, approaching that one solar system in the one part of the galaxy. You get closer and closer... You see the first planet get closer to you. it is massive and you can see just how large it is as you approach it. You can see its beautiful blue form, spinning about, with streaks of other colors within it. It is Neptune, at the edge of the solar system. You get closer and closer to it, breathing deeply as you move.
You breathe in...

One... Two... Three... Four...

And out...

One... Two... Three... Four...

You breathe in...

One... Two... Three... Four...

And out...

One... Two... Three... Four...

Breathing deeply, you can see the surface of Neptune, spinning round and round. You can see it spinning there, brightly shining in the sun's light. It is so far from the sun, and yet you can see it clearly. You can see the color perfectly reflected in the light, even from a distance.

You move past Neptune, and soon, you approach a big planet that is a beautiful blue-green color. It has an icy ring wrapped about it, and you can see it there, shimmering about. You pass it quickly, and move toward Saturn with the next breath.

You breathe in...

One... Two... Three... Four...

And out...

One... Two... Three... Four...

Soon, you're past Jupiter, and the asteroid belt, and with another breath, you pass Mars.

You breathe in...

One... Two... Three... Four...

And out...

One... Two... Three... Four...

Then, you approach Earth, getting closer and closer to see the bright blue water, and the green land, but you're careful not to get too close. You recognize the home there, but you choose not to get too close. You pass by and take a big, deep breath again.
You breathe in...

One... Two... Three... Four...

And out...

One... Two... Three... Four...

Soon, you pass Venus, and Mercury too, and you go all the way past the sun as well, and before long, you have left the solar system. Just like that, you're leaving it behind. You're growing. You're getting bigger and bigger. You're going further and further from your home, and soon, you are away from all things familiar. You lost, but you are not afraid. You are exploring the universe all around you and you are loving every moment of it. You feel like you do not have a care in the world.

You are a star. You are brightly burning as your inner flame grows larger and larger. You feel it spreading out, engulfing you, and granting you that endless peace within yourself. It protects you. It burns away your troubles, and as you burn, you realize that there are very few troubles that a star can have. You are safe. You are able to embrace yourself.

You feel at peace. As you leave behind the home that you know, you feel yourself growing bigger and bigger. You leave behind your troubles with the solar system, and the further you get away from them, the more you see that they are smaller and less significant than you thought. You have left behind all of the trouble. You have left behind all of the pain and the stress. The further you flow into the universe, the more at peace you feel. You have left them all behind, all of your stressors and you feel your body beginning to relax more and more.

You breathe in...

One... Two... Three... Four...

And out...

One... Two... Three... Four...

You grow bigger and bigger as you go further away. You see a comet in the air. It leaves a trail of icy dust in its path. You can see it sparkling. You can see it glowing. You can see it flying through the universe. Slowly at first. You can see it flowing slowly. It's so slow that it looks like it isn't moving at first, but the trail of ice it leaves shows that even it is not stagnant. It is moving about. It is flowing through space and time, just like you are.

You are made of the same cosmic dust as the comet right in front of you. You are just as profound, just as unique, and just as wondrous as comet is. You are connected to the stars as a part of the same universe and when you look at the grand scheme of the universe, those problems of your day suddenly aren't so big after all. You can find peace in this sort of revelation and any time you need to, you can return to this inner cosmic world for yourself. it will help you.

You breathe in...

One... Two... Three... Four...

And out...

One... Two... Three... Four...

You breathe in...

One... Two... Three... Four...

And out...

One... Two... Three... Four...

Just as you grew into the great, big cosmic body, you find yourself shrinking back down again. You find yourself back in your usual human self. You find yourself floating there, in that great, big nothingness. You see yourself there, drifting comfortably through the space. You are at peace with yourself.

You know that you can leave behind your problems. You know that the problems might seem big when you're in the moment, but they can be left behind. You become aware of yourself in the moment in your bed. You are perfectly comfortable and content. You visualize that everything around your bed, in your room, is far, far from the outside world, and you feel at peace.

Your room is your special refuge, away from the outside world and the outside troubles. You can protect yourself when you are within your room and it is the perfect environment for sleep. Where you are is perfect to help you get a nice, full night, and you know it.

You feel yourself getting sleepier now as you drift on your bed. You are there, floating and waiting. You are there, relaxing and enjoying the moment. You are there and you can forget your stressors as you rest. You can allow yourself to get further and further away from Earth and from your problems, just by looking within yourself.

You breathe in...

One... Two... Three... Four...

And out...

One... Two... Three... Four...

You are feeling too sleepy to resist now. You can feel yourself getting heavy. You do not float about as much anymore, and you can feel yourself sinking into your bed, deeper and deeper. You feel yourself comfortable and ready to sleep. You can feel yourself forgive yourself for any problems form the day. You can feel yourself let go of your worries. You can feel yourself distance yourself further and further from them, welcoming only peace and love within yourself.

Your eyes feel heavy and your mind feels slow.

You breathe in...

One... Two... Three... Four...

And out...

One... Two... Three... Four...

You feel ready to sleep once and for all and you welcome it. You open your mind and your boy to the rest that awaits you. You welcome the peace and joy it will bring you.

You breathe in...

One... Two... Three... Four...

And out...

One... Two... Three... Four...

You breathe in...

One... Two... Three... Four...

And out...

One... Two... Three... Four...

You are at peace and you are finally falling asleep. Good night and rest well.

Guided Meditation 2: Peaceful Paradise

In this guided meditation, you will be transported to a world far from home, where you are able to find total serenity. Surrounded by ivory sand and cerulean water, with the crystal clear sky and a verdant green rainforest, you will be invited to explore your surroundings, to let your anxiety and stress melt away under the tropical sun and the blanket of the forest canopy, and allow yourself a moment to breathe in total relaxation to help you gently fall asleep before you know it.

Close your eyes and take in a big, deep breath. Feel the air flowing through your nose. Notice how it feels. Focus in the temperature and the smells. Feel it filling up your lungs, with your lungs swelling up within you like great, big balloons in your chest until you feel like they can't swell up any more. Feel the air warming in your chest and exhale slowly, feeling the air pass your lips gently and slowly. Is it warm? With each breath that you take, you feel yourself calming down.

You breathe in... And out...

Now, feel yourself. Focus on your center, the point just above your belly button. How does it feel? Is it tense? Tight? Stressed? Focus on this point as you inhale in. One... Two... Three... Four... Five... and out... One... Two... three... Four... Five... Focus on that spot for another breath or two...

Now, feel the tension in your body. Become aware of any tension you are holding in your head and face. As you breathe in, imagine that you are pushing the tension down to the center above your belly button. Let it gather there. Now, feel the tension in your shoulders. Focus on that stress and tension and as you breathe in, feel it moving down to your center. Let it gather there, imagining your tension and stress all becoming balled up in the center. Feel the tension in your arms and hands gathering and flowing in to your center. Feel that center growing with the tension and allow it to build up. Then, take the tension from your chest and upper back, and flow it down toward your center.

Then, go down to your toes and feet, identifying the tension that is there. Push it up, feeling it flowing up your legs, through your pelvis and belly, and noting it as it arrives in the belly. Focus on it as it grows within you and allow it to flow.

Feel all of the tension in your body and imagine it turning into a flame within you. Imagine it flickering and burning within your belly, but as it burns, it is released into the world. You burn the tension more and more, helping it to release itself out of you. You reject the tension that was within you and push it to your inner core so you can allow it all to dissipate. You want to be relaxed and with every moment of burning within yourself, you find yourself relaxing more and more. Your head starts to relax and you feel your stress fading away. Your shoulders and your arms begin to relax and the fire in your belly comfortably burns it away. Your tension in your chest fades and you feel incredibly warm and comfortable. Finally, the tension from the other side begins to burn off as well, leaving your entire body entirely at ease and completely relaxed. You have released all of your tension and are left with a small, bright flame in your stomach, flickering along with your heart. With every beat, it crackles within you, helping you to stay relaxed.

With every exhale, you breathe out what was left of your tension. It gathers in your lungs with your used air. It all gathers up into one place for simple burning and you will be able to help yourself to stay relaxed. You can draw on this flame whenever you find yourself stressed with tension. Whenever you feel the need to alleviate the stress within you, you can focus on the tension and burn it within yourself, imagining as it all toasts up and burns away.

You now have space within yourself to welcome relaxation and positivity.

Breathe in... One... Two... Three... Four... Five... And out... One... Two... Three... Four... Five... As you breathe in, imagine the feeling of relaxation flowing within you, emanating from your inner fire throughout your body. Feel it in your head. Breathe in... and out... Feel the relaxation pulsating in your shoulders and arms... Feel it spreading throughout your chest. Feel it spread down to your legs and feet. It fills your whole body, bringing you utter peace and relaxation. Your mind feels incredibly open and ready to go on a peaceful, relaxing adventure. Your body is ready to fall deeper and deeper into your relaxation so you can become more and more relaxed.

As you relax, you realize that your feet have sunk into sand. It is warm, yet soft and smooth. The sand is wonderful underneath you—you love every step that you take within it. When you look down, you see that the sand is a beautiful ivory color and it spreads out in front of you for what seems like forever. It glistens in the noonday sunlight, shimmering and sparkling as the light catches the sides of the crystals.

You look to the right and see the brightest, clearest, bluest water you have ever seen, cerulean in color. The top is rippling with white reflections of light as the water shifts about. It is nearly still, save for mild rippling. The gentle waves lapped at the sand, leaving lines of wetness, darkening the sand as they pulled back toward the sea. It was an endless dance—the water comes in, spraying at the sand, and the water pulls back out, receding. It goes back and forth and you watch it calmly, breathing gently.

You breathe in...

One... Two... Three... Four...

And out...

One... Two... Three... Four...

Above you, the sky is nearly as deep a blue as the ocean. It is perfectly clear with just a few stray wisps of clouds drifting about. It is the perfect day for a beachside adventure and you are free to enjoy it however you would like to do. You are free to settle down and nap in the sun, enjoying the warmth, or you can choose to walk and explore. You could swim, or you could rest. What you do with yourself is up to you.

You breathe in...

One... Two... Three... Four...

And out...

One... Two... Three... Four...

You hear the distant cries of seagulls warbling in the ocean air. They sound shrill and high as they circle above the water. They are perfectly content to keep on circling above. You watch them lazily glide along the breeze that brings with it the scent of salt and kelp with a hint of fishiness included. It is a beautiful day to relax and you intend to do so. As you bask in the sunlight, you feel yourself radiating calmness.

Listen to your mind for a moment. Let yourself focus inwardly on it and experience where it stands. Do you feel any anxiety in the moment? Are you worried about something that you need to do in the next few days? Are you stressing out about something that is going to be less than fun?

You breathe in...

One... Two... Three... Four...

And out...

One... Two... Three... Four...

As you exhale, you feel your worries starting to fade away. They are starting to melt out of your body as you breathe. The more that you breathe, the more capable of calming yourself down you become. You feel empowered. You feel in control. You know that as you continue to breathe, you'll feel even better than before.

You breathe in...

One... Two... Three... Four...

And out...

One... Two... Three... Four...

You can see the line between the sand and the soil, where the plants start growing on the island. You can see the vivid, brightly colored foliage sprouting from the trees. Fronds of palm and coconut sway gently in the breeze, rustling together and creating an air of serenity about you. You can hear them creating a gentle, rhythmic sound as they rub together, and all around you, you can hear the sounds of hundreds of birds, all singing together. There are trilling birds and there are more loud screeching birds. There are birds that sound so faint that you can barely hear them, and there are birds that sound like they are right above you—because they are.

When you look up, you see a flurry of birds, fluttering from branch to branch, from tree to tree. They are beautiful and in every color imaginable. There are some that are so black, they look like they are impossible to see. There are some that are blue and green. There are big birds and small. They are each unique in their own ways. They all have their own specific look, but each one is worthy of your attention.

You decide to walk toward the birds, feeling the sand underneath your feet slowly change. Step by step, you approach that point of foliage on the island and soon, you are there, standing on the edge between where the beach meet the trees. You can see them all lined out there, creating a sort of wall. You can feel that the air is cooler there—it is still just as humid, but it is noticeably lower with the shade of the trees. You look back over your shoulder, seeing that there is the whole expanse of beach to explore, and you turn to keep going deeper. You walk further into the wooded area. You can see that there is a rich, fertile soil underfoot, perhaps from the volcano that once brought this island into existence. You can see it, dark and lush. You can feel how soft the soil is underfoot as well as you step, one by one. Despite the shade, it is warm underneath your feet.

You breathe in...

One... Two... Three... Four...

And out...

One... Two... Three... Four...

Look around yourself for a moment. You can see the bright green leaves just about everywhere around you. They come in ferns and in leaves. They come large and sall. Some have vines draped between them, dangling as long tendrils that weave in and out between the leaves, almost creating a tapestry between them. They are covered in leaves, and even the occasional frog that you can spot if you look closely.

You continue to walk through the small forest, looking around yourself and absorbing it all it. It is gorgeous, peaceful, and so compelling to walk through. You find yourself in awe with the beauty. You find yourself shocked at just how diverse the area is. You can see butterflies hovering and fluttering their way across the forest. They come in every color, but one catches your eye.

The butterfly is massive—easily the size of your hand if you were to outstretch all of your fingers. It is almost brown in color as it sits there on the plant. It has what looks like spotted eyes amongst its wingspan, and there are areas that are darker and almost barred. The color is reminiscent of a tiger's own stripes and there are a wide array of different shades present among the butterfly's wings.

You breathe in...

One... Two... Three... Four...

And out...

One... Two... Three... Four

You look closer at the butterfly, leaning in, and you can suddenly see its six long legs clinging to the length of a vine. You can see the great, big black eyes that stare back up at you, almost beadily. The antennae atop the butterfly's head quiver, picking up signals about the world that you will never understand.

The butterfly opens up its wings and suddenly, you are treated with a view of the bright sunset-colored wings that were hidden when they were folded up on its back. They shimmer in a ray of sunlight that falls through the canopy. The centermost part of the butterfly, closest to its body, is a beautiful white color, fading into yellow, then golden, and orange, with the bottommost wings a deep black. It was a beautiful butterfly—a sunset morpho butterfly, and with its wings spread out as much as they could be, you realize that it is much larger than your hand when you outstretch it. Its wings fold up and down slowly.

You realize that the butterfly there is not alone—there are many more of them, all sitting atop the vines. There are some in different colors. Your eyes find one that, when it opens up its wings to reveal the outsides of them, is the most brilliant blue that you have ever seen. The wings appeared black and soft before they were opened—with eye spots of black, yellow, and violet along their surfaces, but as soon as the wings are unfurled, you see them for what they are—that azure color that rivals that of the ocean that you have just seen. You see the blue appear to shimmer almost iridescently in the filtered light, and then, suddenly and unexpectedly, all of the butterflies take flight.

There are hundreds of them flying past you, in every color that you can see. They are wonderful as they flutter by, and you can feel yourself, your heart, growing lighter as they leave. One by one, they take away that negativity, that anxiety, and your apprehensions about the world. They leave you feeling more comfortable, calmer, and more willing to see the world as a kind, friendly place. They take away your fear as they fly by and as you watch them, slowly disappearing into your surroundings, you feel at peace. You feel at ease. You feel ready to commit to your own peace of mind and you embrace it.

You breathe in...

One... Two... Three... Four...

And out...

One... Two... Three... Four

You feel your peace and clarity within yourself and as you do, you realize that the clarity is freeing. You feel free within yourself. You are free from the troubles that you have. You are free from the struggles of your world and you are at peace. You are comfortable and relaxed. You are right where you should be in the moment.

You keep heading through the tropical forest. In the distance, you can hear what sounds like monkeys in the distance. Their voices are shrill, and yet jubilant all at the same time. They are happy in their cheers and they sound like they are heading toward you. You head toward them as well, curious about what made up the sound. You want to know why they are all squealing the way that they are and you head toward them, searching for the source of the sound. You keep your eyes up above you, scanning about the canopy in hopes of finding the source of the sound. You know that there must be monkeys running about somewhere. You know that they are probably having a grand time, swinging from branch to branch, so carefree and happy. You can have that same carefree nature, simply learning to trust yourself.

Soon, you hear the sounds get louder and louder, and when you look up, you realize that there is a tree full of little, black monkeys. They swing from tree to tree, clinging to the branches with their long, curling tails. They you will be able to see you as they swing about and they are watching you. Their cries slow down as they notice you, and one of them gets closer. It swings down, branch to branch, until it reaches a thick vine, and it slides down to look at you. It gets into your face and leans in closely.

The monkey is not very big—it is furry and black with a hairless face with big eyes. The eyes look up at you. The monkey is hanging upside down as it watches you, holding on to the tree with its long tail. Its hands look remarkably human as it watches you, eyes unfathomable. You look back into its eyes and feel calm. You feel content. You understand it as you both gaze into each other's eyes. You sense that the monkey wants you to follow it as it watches you, and you are happy to do so. You feel compelled to go with it, and without having to say a word, the monkey seems to understand.

The monkey leaves you, climbing back up the tree effortlessly. It flies up with ease, climbing as if it were easier than anything it had ever done before. It waits at the top, turning back to meet your gaze, and you understand. You must follow the monkey to see where it wants to take you. Just as suddenly, the monkey begins to move, swinging from branch to branch. It is slower now than it was earlier, and you know that it is moving slower for you. You slowly make your way to follow them, never letting your eyes off of them as you walk along the ground.

You have to dodge trees and climb over roots as you go, but you do it anyway. You don't think about how hard it will be for you to do so—your mind is simply focused on what you are going to do. You are going to follow those monkeys and see where they go. They must know the best places to go, you tell yourself. They know where to go and what to do. This is their home, and you are eager to see what it looks like.

You dodge vines and slip underneath ferns. You ignore the butterflies. You ignore the birds that sing their songs around you. All you focus on is the monkeys in front of you and your breath as you go. Your breathing is a bit quicker, but not strained as you go. As the monkeys pick up their speed, you pick up your own as well. You keep going for what feels like an eternity.

Breathe in...

One... Two... Three... Four...

And out...

One... Two... Three... Four.

Suddenly, the monkeys stop. And, when you look around, you realize that they have taken you deeply into the rainforest. You can barely see through the canopy and it is much darker where you are. The monkeys are quiet and when you look up at them, you realize that all eyes are on you, watching you as you sit there in their home. They want to know what you are going to do next.

You breathe in...

One... Two... Three... Four...

And out...

One... Two... Three... Four.

You realize that you can hear the dull roar of water where you are. You can hear it babbling as it flows from somewhere... And when you look around, you realize where it was coming from. It was coming from a small waterfall, babbling over a cliff into a small stream. The rocks are black and craggy where they are and the water seems to fall from them in a million different directions, spraying little drops of water everywhere. The water is shallow as it falls down the rocks, cascading gently. You are in awe of the water—it is crystal clear and you can see right down to the bottom. There are little frogs and tadpoles swimming about in the shallowest parts, away from the currents created by the waterfall.

You look back at the monkeys and they are still watching you, waiting for your response. It feels almost surreal as you sit there, listening to the water washing over the rocks. You feel at peace where you are looking and you are content. You enjoy the sound and you breathe.

You watch the water for a while. You watch it flowing, and you allow yourself and you feel at peace. You feel like you are able to enjoy the moment. You sit there, looking at the ripples as the water flows. You watch the bubbly froth where it arises at the base of the waterfall, and you feel peaceful. You feel as if your stress and tension fades away. You feel as fluid and free and as light as the water that flows in front of you. you settle down to sit in place for a while. You sit yourself there so that you can enjoy the moment.

The monkeys around you are still quiet, and one by one, they curl up in the trees. You see them cuddling, babies with their mothers, and sometimes a few adults cuddled together peacefully. You see them all, watching the water peacefully and at ease. They watch it flow, listening to the cadence. You are aware of the sound of a bird somewhere in the distance—it is a single bird, trilling and tweeting in the distance. You are aware of it singing happily. You listen closely to it as it does and you feel utterly relaxed.

As you sit there, you are able to free yourself from the stress and anxiety. You tell yourself to stop worrying about the world. You focus inwardly on your breathing now, letting the sound of the water fade to the back of your mind. You feel fully present in the moment.

You tell yourself that you will be just fine. You tell yourself that you are at peace. You are happy.

As you sit there, you become aware of that inner fire within yourself. You focus on what you are doing. You feel how you feel, perfectly at peace. You remind yourself that you are within your perfect moment of peace. You feel good. You feel calm. You take a deep breath.

You breathe in...

One... Two... Three... Four...

And out...

One... Two... Three... Four.

You are at ease. You are content. You can feel yourself growing calmer and at peace as you sit. You feel your body relaxing as you feel at peace. You feel yourself sinking. Your head feels heavy. Your body feels like it is sinking into the ground underneath you. You can feel the waves of sleepiness falling and crashing over you as you sit there. You feel like you are the rocks that the water is washing over.

You breathe in...

One... Two... Three... Four...

And out...

One... Two... Three... Four.

The longer that you sit there, the sleepier you become. The heavier your body feels as you feel ready to drift to sleep. You feel yourself become sleepier and sleepier as you sit there. Listen to the sounds of the forest as you relax more and more. Allow yourself to relax to yourself. Let yourself sink deeper and deeper into relaxation. You have released your anxiety. You have released your tension. Focus inwardly as you listen to the water flowing and the birds singing. Feel your inner fire burning to bring you relaxation. Feel your fire spreading throughout your body, providing you with protection. Your inner fire burns brightly to protect yourself and shields your entire body. It protects you, repelling the stress.

On your perfect paradise, you know that you are shielded. You are far from the stressors of life. You don't have to worry here—life is simpler here. It is relaxing where you stand. You feel your body growing warmer and heavier. Your eyes can barely stay open. You can barely keep yourself awake. You focus on your breathing again.

You breathe in...

One... Two... Three... Four...

And out...

One... Two... Three... Four.

You are getting so close to falling asleep. You stop fighting it. You welcome the peace and quiet. You welcome the peace and quiet that you have in your life. You feel perfectly content.

You are at ease. Your sleepiness washes over you and you are willing to accept it. You embrace it and you drift off to sleep, peacefully, to the lullaby of the world around you.

You breathe in...

One... Two... Three... Four...

And out...

One... Two... Three... Four.

Good night, sleep tight and rest well.

www.ingramcontent.com/pod-product-compliance
Lightning Source LLC
Chambersburg PA
CBHW071516080526
44588CB00011B/1449